Level A

Writing Workshop

Senior Series Consultant
Beverly Ann Chin
Professor of English
University of Montana
Missoula, MT

Series Consultant
Frederick J. Panzer, Sr.
English Dept. Chair, Emeritus
Christopher Columbus High School
Miami, FL

Series Editor
Phyllis Goldenberg

Sadlier

Credits

Cover Art and Design
William H. Sadlier, Inc. and Studio Montage

Interior Photos
istock International Inc/ Elementallmaging: 74; Eriklam: 41; Lovleah: 29; LindaYolanda: 60; Syntika: 28. Jupiterimages Corporation/AbleStock.com 107; BananaStock Image: 82, 97; Brand X Pictures: 77; Comstock Images: 7, 58, 84, 93; Creatas Images: 4, 9, 17; Liquidlibrary Image: 90; PhotoObjects.net: 25; Photos.com: 49, 70, 72, 101, 110; Thinkstock Images: 21, 48, 50; Library of Congress, New York: New York City W.P.A. Art Project: 114; Shutterstock Images/Alexey Avdeev: 78; Katrina Brown: 14; Comstock Images: 33; Mike Flippo: 5, 44; Alexandar Iotzov: 46; Rafa Irusta: 86; Eric Isselée: 20; markrhiggins: 55; philophoto: 65; pjmorley: 66; Glenda M. Powers: 38; Leah-Anne Thompson: 75.

Previously published as *Composition Workshop* © 1996, 1994 by Herbert M. Rothstein.

Printed in the United States of America

Student Edition: ISBN: 978-0-8215-8506-1
2 3 4 5 6 7 8 9 / 13 12 11 10 09

Dear Student,

Whether you are writing an essay for school or writing an e-mail to a friend, you can only get your message across if you write clearly and correctly. ***Writing Workshop*** can help you improve your writing skills in an interesting and easy-to-understand way.

Writing Workshop begins by introducing you to the basics. First, you'll learn how to write **clear and effective sentences.** After you master the structure of sentences, you'll move on to writing **paragraphs.** Finally, you'll learn how to produce many different **types of writing** that you'll need to use in school, on tests, and in life. In addition, you will learn how to write for **different purposes,** such as to explain, persuade, describe, entertain, and convey an experience. This way, you will be prepared for any writing assignment that comes your way.

Don't worry. ***Writing Workshop*** will guide you along the way, offering **tips and clear instructions** that tell you exactly what to do and how to do it. For example, grammar tips remind you about important grammar rules and provide easy-to-understand explanations. **Tech Tips** guide you for writing on computers. Also, the writing workshop chapters end with a complete **Writing Model** that shows you exactly what a strong essay looks like.

Throughout the book, you'll have plenty of opportunities **to practice** each new skill you learn. As this program will show you, writing doesn't have to be done alone. Many activities will ask you to work with a **partner or in a small group.** As you develop your skills, **writing prompt** activities allow you to show off your writing and put to use the techniques you have learned.

Writing Workshop will give you a strong set of writing skills that you can use in school and throughout your life. With ***Writing Workshop***, you'll become a better and more confident writer.

Good Luck!

The Authors

CONTENTS

CONTENTS *continued*

THE WRITING PROCESS

PREWRITING

Finding an Idea

- Freewrite or brainstorm ideas for a topic.
- Choose and narrow a topic.
- Gather details in a list or a graphic organizer.

Making a Plan

- Define your purpose.
- Know your audience.
- Put your details in order.

DRAFTING

- Concentrate on getting your ideas down—*not* on fixing errors!
- Keep your reader in mind as you write.
- Write a complete beginning, middle, and end.

REVISING

- Review your draft, looking for ways to improve it.
- As you review your draft, focus on five of the six traits of good writing (ideas and content, organization, sentence fluency, word choice, and voice).
- Ask a peer reviewer to give feedback on your draft.

EDITING AND PROOFREADING

- Look for mistakes in the sixth trait of good writing, conventions (grammar, usage, mechanics, and spelling).
- Proofread your draft one last time.

PUBLISHING AND PRESENTING

- Write a final version of your paper.
- Share your writing with your audience.

1

Writers at Work

This chapter will help you make your writing clear, correct, and interesting. Effective writing will help you at school, at work, and at home. When you write for others, use the five steps of the writing process: prewriting, drafting, revising, editing and proofreading, and publishing and presenting.

LESSON 1 Prewriting

In the first step of the process, prewriting, you think about what you are writing, why you are writing, and for whom you are writing. Then you choose a topic and gather details.

During prewriting, think about. . .

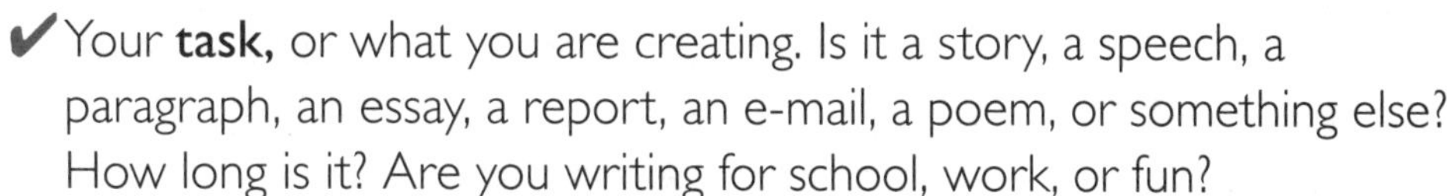

✔ Your **task,** or what you are creating. Is it a story, a speech, a paragraph, an essay, a report, an e-mail, a poem, or something else? How long is it? Are you writing for school, work, or fun?

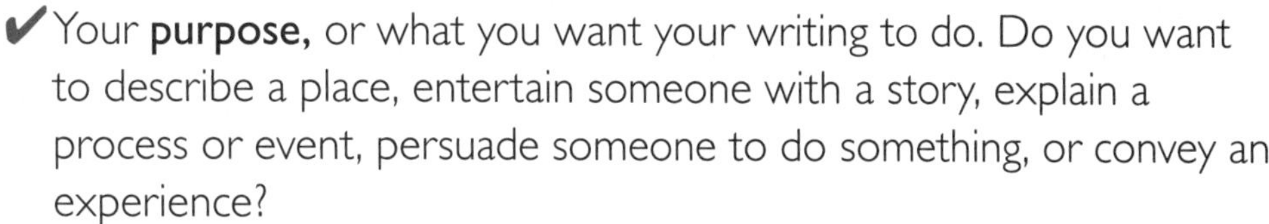

✔ Your **purpose,** or what you want your writing to do. Do you want to describe a place, entertain someone with a story, explain a process or event, persuade someone to do something, or convey an experience?

✔ Your **audience,** or the people who will read your writing. What does your audience already know about your topic? How might they feel about it? Are there certain terms or details that you will need to explain?

When you are searching for a **topic** for your paper, see where your interests lead you. Pick a topic that you truly want to write about. If you are having trouble thinking of the right topic, try using the techniques on the next page.

Ways of Coming Up with Possible Topics

- freewriting
- keeping a writer's notebook
- making a cluster diagram or other graphic organizer
- making a list
- talking with friends or classmates

When you **freewrite,** write anything that comes into your head for a short period of time (about three minutes). Don't worry about grammar or spelling.

Freewriting Model

Notice how the writer doesn't have to use correct grammar or show connections between thoughts.

> What can I write about?—school, school, school, let's see—I like vacations but if there were no school I'd be bored—friends, best friends—schoolwork, homework, hate studying for tests—teachers—teachers who are funny—funny classmates—classmates who are hard to get along with—fitting in—wanting respect, hating being laughed at—teachers always talking about peer pressure—Do I experience peer pressure?

Ideas for topics can come any time from anywhere, such as news items, conversations, and observations. Keep a writer's notebook to collect ideas for future reference.

Sample Writer's Notebook Page

> 4/12/09
> I read an article in the newspaper about foreign elections. How are foreign elections different from U.S. elections?
>
> 4/20/09
> I had a dream about being deep underwater but still able to breathe. Good idea for a story.
>
> 5/02/09
> I can't go to an amusement park because I have to babysit for my brother. I'd like to write a speech about how unfair it is.

When you **cluster,** you use a graphic organizer to record whatever thoughts and ideas come to mind. Cluster diagrams can help you see connections among your ideas as you explore topics. If you don't want to make a graphic organizer, you can simply list your ideas.

Tip

Narrow your topic to make it more specific and manageable. Notice how the writer starts with a broad topic and increasingly narrows it.

A Cluster on the Subject of "Sports"

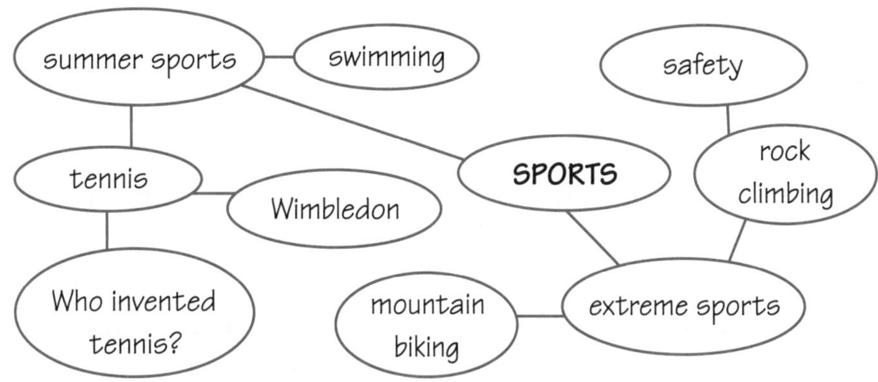

After you narrow your topic, gather details by. . .

- clustering or listing what you already know about your topic
- clustering or listing what you think people would want to know about your topic
- finding more information on your topic by going to the library to research, checking an encyclopedia, accessing the Internet, or talking with an expert

Before you go further in the writing process, ask yourself the following questions. If you have trouble answering any of them, revise your topic or choose a new one.

✔ Have I decided exactly what my topic is? Can I sum it up in one sentence?

✔ Do I know what my purpose is?

✔ Do I know who my audience is?

✔ Do I know what form my writing will take—essay, poem, presentation, something else?

✔ Is the topic appropriate for the length of the assignment I am writing?

✔ Am I truly interested in this topic?

Activity A

With a partner, use one of the methods given in this lesson to come up with possible topics for each situation given below. Show your work on a separate sheet of paper. Remember to narrow your topic as you prewrite.

1. **Situation:** Your English teacher wants you to write an essay that describes your favorite vacation.

2. **Situation:** Your science teacher wants you to write a research report about an animal.

3. **Situation:** Your social studies teacher wants you to make a brochure that persuades people to visit a historic site.

Activity B

Imagine you are going to write a paragraph informing your teacher of your views on a particular topic. Choose one of the broad subjects listed below. Decide on a narrower topic that interests you, write it below, and explain why you chose it.

- games
- the environment
- computers/technology
- health

Narrow topic: ____

____

Why I chose it: ____

____

____

____

Activity C

Now gather details about the topic you chose in Activity B. Use the methods described in this lesson to gather the information you would use in writing your paragraph.

LESSON  Drafting

Your goal in writing a first draft is to take your ideas from the prewriting stage and write them down in a way that is organized enough to make sense to readers.

Starting to put your thoughts down on paper can seem a bit scary. That's why it's helpful to remember that a first draft is only an attempt to get your ideas down.

Before you write your first draft, ask yourself. . .

✔ Do I know enough about my topic to begin writing? (If not, you should research more before you begin.)

✔ What is the focus of my writing? What am I talking about, and what do I want to do?

✔ Who do I think will read my writing?

✔ What background information might my reader need?

✔ How can I best present the information I have?

Tip

You will make changes to your draft in the next stage of writing, so write on every other line and leave wide margins. This will let you make corrections.

Try to present your details in a way that you think will be effective, but remember that you can always change your organization later. Your work will be very different by the time it is ready to be turned in. Be sure, though, that you write a complete essay when you draft.

A complete essay includes

- an **introduction,** which gets your readers' attention and tells them what your essay will be about and your opinion on that topic (your thesis)
- a **body** made up of middle paragraphs that support your thesis
- a **conclusion** that restates the major ideas from your essay and leaves the reader with something to think about

Drafting DOs and DON'Ts

✔ DO consider going back to the prewriting stage if you find that your topic is too broad, too narrow, not a good fit for the task, or not something you want to spend time writing about.

✔ DO write down every thought you have, even if you might not end up using all of them.

✔ DO jump from idea to idea. Only you have to be able to follow your train of thought. You can improve organization when you revise.

✔ DON'T worry about correct spelling, grammar, and usage. In the next stages—revising and editing—you will fix any errors you might have made.

✔ DON'T feel that you have to write the beginning first. Begin by writing whatever is easiest and clearest for you, no matter if it's the middle or even the end.

✔ DON'T try to imitate anyone when you write. Use a tone appropriate to your task and audience, but write in your own voice.

Activity A **Imagine that you want to persuade your family to get a dog. Below are some notes. Use them to write a persuasive paragraph. Arrange the ideas in a sensible order. Then, on a separate sheet of paper, write a paragraph that states your case. When you have finished, trade papers with a peer and see if he or she finds your paragraph convincing.**

- I'm old enough now to be responsible for a pet.
- Dogs can guard the house and protect kids.
- Dogs are very friendly and affectionate.
- In shelters, many abandoned dogs are kept in small cages.
- We'd be saving a dog's life if we adopted one.
- I would learn about being grown up and having to take care of someone else.

Activity B **On a separate sheet of paper, write a first draft of a paragraph based on the topic and details you gathered in Activities B and C of Lesson 1.**

LESSON 3

Revising

Revising is the most important step in the writing process. When you revise, you evaluate, or judge, your draft based on five of the six traits of good writing. You make changes to improve your draft.

Tip

The sixth writing trait, ***conventions,*** *includes grammar, usage, mechanics, punctuation, and spelling. You'll check for these things during the next stage of the writing process (editing and proofreading). Be prepared to make major changes. The revising stage is the only chance you'll have to significantly improve your paper.*

During revision, you should focus on the **five traits of good writing.**

Trait	General Questions to Ask as You Revise
Ideas and Content	• Does my writing focus on the topic? • What information does my reader need? • Could I give more specific details? • Are all of my points related to my topic?
Organization	• Can I use transition words to make clear connections between my ideas? • Do I present my ideas in a logical order? • Does my writing have a beginning, middle, and end?
Voice	• Have I tried to sound like anyone else? • How can I make my writing sound more like me?
Word Choice	• Can I add precise words that reduce confusion? • Can I use words that better express my meaning?
Sentence Fluency	• How can I make my writing easier to read? • How can I make my writing more interesting to read?

The kinds of changes you make while revising depend on your purpose, your audience, and the form of your writing.

Specific Questions for Narrative Writing

- How natural does the dialogue sound?
- How clearly have I connected each piece of action to the next?
- How detailed are my descriptions of characters and setting?

Specific Questions for Persuasive Writing

- How clearly have I stated my opinion on the topic?
- How convincing are the reasons I give to take the action I recommend?
- What might someone who disagrees with my opinion say? How can I address or disprove that person's arguments?

Specific Questions for Expository Writing

- How interesting is my introduction?
- How many main ideas do I have in each paragraph?
- How many details support each main idea?
- Could I do more research to explain something better?
- Can I write a stronger conclusion?

Below is an example of a revised paragraph that explains how to get a horse ready to ride.

Leave room between lines to make additions, notes, and changes.

Delete unrelated details.

Add details.

¶You have to follow several steps when getting a horse ready to ride.
^The first thing you do is comb out the horse's coat with a round brush. ~~A horse's coat gets matted with dirt.~~ Then you brush the coat again with a soft brush to make it shine. ~~It's a good idea to wash off the horse after you ride if it's very hot outside.~~ After brushing, you can put on the blanket ~~on its back~~. Then put the saddle on and ^tighten the girth ^so the saddle stays in place. ~~which is tightened.~~ Finally, You put on the bridle. Get in the saddle, and away you go!

Peer reviewing is a tool you can use during the revising step. You can exchange your papers.

Activity A **The following paragraph was written for a school newspaper. Revise it to add more specific information and to correct any other problems. You may use the information from the notes below, or you can create more details to include. Start your revision on this page. Copy your revised paragraph onto a clean sheet of paper.**

Recycling is a pretty good idea for a lot of reasons. What can we do at school? There are home recycling programs. Students can collect things. We can put recycling bins in places around school. What should we collect? Someone should be in charge of the project, it could be a teacher or a student. Or maybe a committee.

Notes

- Reasons for recycling—saves resources, keeps Earth cleaner
- Plan of action: First, decide what to recycle. Glass, aluminum, paper
- Recycling bins in cafeteria, hallway next to the principal's office, outside the school
- Appoint student and teacher in charge of recycling project, or a committee of volunteers to work with teacher
- What those in charge will do: request weekly pickup from recycling truck, figure out who will empty recycling bins and where and how to store recycled material

Activity B **Compare your revised paragraph to those of other students. Discuss the similarities and the differences in the revisions each of you made. What revisions did you make? Why did you make those revisions?**

LESSON 4 Editing and Proofreading

When you edit and proofread, you check for errors in the sixth writing trait, conventions. First edit your paper for usage, making changes to confirm that all your sentences are correct and clear. Then proofread your work to correct any mistakes in spelling, punctuation, mechanics, and grammar.

Tip

The editing and proofreading stage of the writing process makes your writing error free, polished, and readable. Error-free writing always makes a good impression.

Tips for Editing

- Read your work aloud. If any of your sentences read awkwardly, edit to make them smoother.
- Have a friend or family member read your work. Ask him or her to tell you if any of your sentences seem incorrect or unclear.
- Check each pronoun in a sentence (*he, she, it, they*) to be sure it clearly refers to the specific noun you want it to.
- Make sure all your sentences are complete. Each should have at least one noun and one verb and should express a complete thought.

Proofreading Symbols

mississippi river	Capitalize.
the River	Make lowercase.
went to bed ¶The next day,	Start a new paragraph.
has not been dif f icult	Add.
inside of the cabin	Delete.
Dr Payne is here	Add a period.
Sincerely yours ,	Add a comma.
The bell rang ; the class left.	Add a semicolon.
here come wierd	Switch order.
ice # cream	Add a space.
a base ball cap	Close up space.

The inside back cover of this book shows even more proofreading marks. For capitalization and punctuation rules, see the Writer's Handbook at the back of this book.

Tips for Proofreading

- Edit your work line by line or sentence by sentence. This practice will help you spot errors you might have missed previously.
- Take some time between editing and proofreading. If you set your work aside for a day, you will be able to see mistakes more easily.
- Have a classmate read your work and mark any mistakes. A fresh set of eyes will catch mistakes you might have missed.

Tech Tip

Your teacher will probably ask you to double-space your work. This will give you enough room to mark corrections in your work. You can change spacing under your "Format" menu.

Example of a Proofread Paragraph

At the Movies

You have ~~has~~ to judge just the right time to get to the movies. If you get there too early, there's ~~theirs~~ too much time to wait for the show to start. if you get there too ~~to~~ late, ~~then~~ the line is too long at the popcorn and candy concession, so ~~and~~ you have to hold all your friends' places in line ~~for them~~ while they race off to play the video games. ~~and~~ you don't get to play any at all. ~~And~~ even if you are ~~your~~ the championship player and play really well, ~~good~~, you don't even get ~~got~~ a chance to try. So my advice is to get there just about fifteen minutes before the show starts. ~~and~~ a good idea is to take along a little brother or sister to hold your place in line for popcorn!

After you have finished editing and proofreading, make a clean final copy, with no corrections remaining.

Proofreading Checklist

- ✔ Check for misspelled words, including words your computer's spell-checker might have missed.
- ✔ Make sure all your paragraphs are indented.
- ✔ Check that each of your sentences starts with a capital letter.
- ✔ Make sure each sentence ends in an end punctuation mark (a period, a question mark, or an exclamation point).

Activity A **Now it's your turn. Below is the retelling of an ancient Roman myth about the origin of spiders. The paragraph is filled with mistakes in grammar, spelling, punctuation, and capitalization. Use the proofreading symbols to mark corrections.**

Arachne Spins Her Web

There once lived a beautiful girl named Arachne who could weave better than anyone else in her village. Unfortunately, she also loved to boaste about the beauty of her work One day the goddess Athena, dressed as an old woman, came to see them and Athena challenged arachne to a weaving contest. Both women begans to weave at once. Though Athena judged the girls cloth to be even more beautifull than his, she knew Arachne needed to be taught a lessen. the goddess sentenced Arachne to be turned into a spider. Ever after, because of Arachne's pride, all spiders has had to live inside its web.

Activity B **Now make a clean copy of your proofread, edited version of the paragraph. Exchange paragraphs with a partner and discuss the changes you made while editing and proofreading.**

LESSON 5

Publishing and Presenting

After you have finished your writing, you publish and present it, which means sharing it with an audience. You should also keep a writer's portfolio for yourself.

Often, you will publish your assigned work by turning it in to your teacher. You should know, however, that you can publish or present your writing in many places besides class. Try searching online for contests for writers of your age or for magazines, e-zines, or blogs that accept young people's writing.

Publishing Ideas for Student Writers

- Make a class presentation of your paper.
- Submit an editorial to the school newspaper.
- Submit a story or poem to the class literary magazine.
- Post an interview on a website.
- Enter essay contests sponsored by newspapers and business organizations.
- Send your work to a young writer's conference.
- Publish your own book; have it bound and give it to family and friends.
- Make your own blog.
- Compile and send out a family newsletter.
- Post your work on a library bulletin board.
- Assemble a cast to perform a story or play you wrote.

Keep a **writer's portfolio** with samples of your work. Along with finished, polished pieces, you should include early and incomplete works to show the progress you have made as a writer.

Many times, you will have to present your work to a group of people, such as your class. Use the tips below to prepare you for presentations.

Presenting Tips

- ✔ Practice reading your work out loud several times before presenting it.
- ✔ Have all visual aids, such as photographs, charts, or illustrations, ready before presenting.
- ✔ Speak clearly so that your audience can understand everything you say.
- ✔ Speak slowly so that your audience can follow your thoughts.
- ✔ Do not spend your entire presentation looking at note cards. Look up at your audience as often as you can.
- ✔ Use effective body language. Stand up straight, and make eye contact with audience members.

Activity A **Put together a portfolio of your writing. It can be from this class, from other classes such as social studies and science, or from outside of school. Then answer the questions below, writing your responses on a separate sheet of paper.**

1. Which is your favorite piece? Why?

2. Which piece got the most positive reaction from its audience? Why?

3. Which piece would benefit from revision? How would you revise it?

Activity B **Look at your writing portfolio. For each piece you included, brainstorm a way you could publish it. You can use the list of publishing ideas, search online, consult a resource in a library, or come up with your own ideas.**

Activity C **Choose your favorite idea for publishing a piece from your portfolio and carry it out. It can take some courage to share your work, but one of the most important parts of writing is having an audience read what you write.**

Focusing on Word Choice

Chapter 2

If you are like many people, you've had the experience of saying, "No, no! That's not what I meant at all! You misunderstood me!" When you write, you can avoid misunderstandings by choosing words that express exactly what you want to say. When you choose the right words, your readers understand what you are saying and enjoy the way you say it.

LESSON 1 Be Exact

As you write, choose specific nouns that help readers form sharp, detailed pictures. Avoid general or vague nouns.

Nouns name people, places, things, or ideas. In the examples below, note how the concrete nouns in the second sentence make the meaning clearer.

Tip

Have classmates describe the pictures that your writing creates in their minds. Was your wording precise enough for them to visualize your description?

General We ate *food* at the picnic.

Concrete We ate *turkey sandwiches, fruit salad,* and *blueberry pie* at the picnic.

Help your readers see and hear the action. Add life to your sentences with vivid verbs.

Compare the verbs in the following sentences. Do you see how the vivid verbs in the second and third sentences form different pictures in your mind? Vivid verbs make the meanings more precise.

We *went* up to the door, Li leading the way.

We *crept* up to the door, Li leading the way.

We *marched* up to the door, Li leading the way.

Modifiers are words that describe. Instead of using vague and overused modifiers, such as *bad, nice,* and *great,* try to use precise modifiers, such as *horrible, gentle,* and *fantastic.*

Compare the modifiers in the sentences below.

Tech Tip

Use the thesaurus in your word processing program to look up the modifiers you use. You can see the different attitudes or feelings associated with them. You can even find more precise words to use.

Vague Thank you for the *very nice* book.

Precise Thank you for the *fascinating* book.

When you write, choose your words carefully. For example, would you rather be called *masterful* or *bossy*? The English language is rich in such **synonyms,** or words with similar meanings. Synonyms share a general meaning, but each may suggest a different attitude or feeling. Notice the shades of meaning in these examples.

With a *proud* smile, Ramón held up the huge gold trophy.

With a *haughty* smile, Ramón held up the huge gold trophy.

With a *smug* smile, Ramón held up the huge gold trophy.

Use a thesaurus to find synonyms, and consult a dictionary to make sure your words suggest exactly what you want them to. Choosing your words carefully will help you express your own personal writing style.

Activity A For each sentence below, replace the italicized words with precise words.

1. We watched a *pretty good* movie.

____

2. The runners *came* across the finish line.

____

3. "You did what?" *said* the teacher.

____

4. The documentary on sharks was *very interesting.*

____

5. The campers *had fun* at the barbecue.

____

Activity B Read each sentence. Circle the word in parentheses that better fits the sentence's meaning.

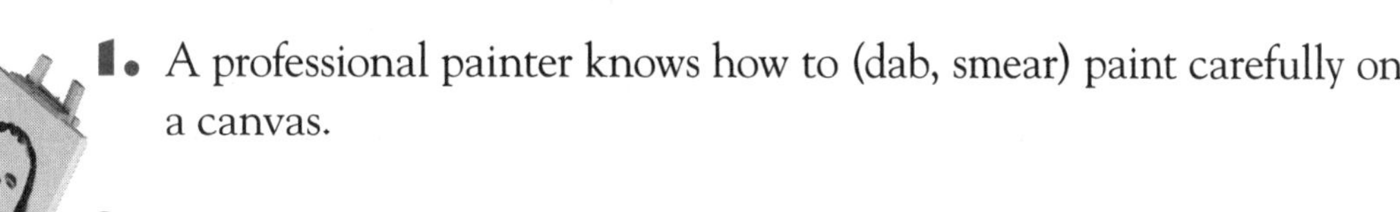

1. A professional painter knows how to (dab, smear) paint carefully on a canvas.

2. After finishing the meal, Viesha (gnawed, pecked) hungrily on a bone.

3. The first astronauts needed to be especially (daring, reckless) because they were venturing into the unknown.

4. "You'll like this (smelly, fragrant) shampoo!" said the hairdresser.

5. People admire José Ortiz because he has been (generous, wasteful) with his wealth.

LESSON 2 Choose the Correct Word

When you are choosing the correct word to express yourself, watch out for homophones and other commonly confused words.

Homophones, or words that sound alike but are spelled differently, can cause confusion for writers. Writers may also be confused by some words that have similar spellings but sound different.

Tip

If you are unsure which homophone to use, look up each homophone in a dictionary. Decide which meaning is the one you want to use.

Commonly Confused Words

its "belonging to it"
it's contraction of *it is* or *it has*

It's time for the dog to take *its* walk.

lose "to be unable to find"; "to fail to win"
loose "not tight"

If the runner's laces are *loose*, he may *lose* the race.

passed past tense of *to pass*
past "over"; "having occurred at an earlier time"

They *passed* the test about events in the *past*.

quiet "making no noise"
quit "to stop"
quite "very much so"

We are not *quite* ready to *quit* working, so please be *quiet*.

their/theirs "belonging to them"
there "in that place"; also used in phrases *there is, there are*
there's contraction of *there is*
they're contraction of *they are*

> *They're* going over *there* to look for *their* coats. *There's* a chance that those coats are *theirs.*

thorough "complete and done with care"
threw past tense of *to throw*
through "in one side and out the other"; "finished with"
though "despite the fact that"; "even if"
thought past tense of *to think*

> We did a *thorough* job when we *threw* out the trash, *though* we *thought* we were not *through* with the cleaning.

weather "temperature, wind, clouds, and other conditions"
whether "if"; used to introduce possibilities

> The *weather* reporter did not say *whether* it would rain.

we're contraction of *we are*
were past tense of *to be* used with plural subject or *you*
where "at that place"
wear "to have on the body"; "to show"; "to damage through use"

> *Where were* you this morning? *We're* always waiting for you to find something to *wear.*

who's contraction of *who is*
whose "belonging to whom or which"

> *Who's* going to tell me *whose* name is on this building?

Activity **Circle the word in parentheses that belongs in each sentence.**

1. The Wongs believe that the black poodle at the pound may be (theirs, there's).

2. (It's, Its) collar is missing, so they can't be sure.

3. If (it's, its) too late for you to talk, I'll call back tomorrow.

4. "(We're, Were, Where) hungry!" complained the children.

5. The neighbors got together to plan (they're, their, there) block party.

6. The class included several students (who's, whose) parents had come from Mexico.

7. The detectives did a (through, thorough) search of the house.

8. Do you know (whose, who's) performing at the concert?

9. Deserts are regions (were, where, we're) rain rarely falls.

10. Mr. and Mrs. Ramos have asked us to come with them.
Is (their, there, they're) room in (their, there, they're) car for us?

11. Do you remember your first (loose, lose) tooth?

12. Rona spent a (quit, quite, quiet) afternoon at home reading a novel.

13. The scientists (thought, though, through) about the problem day and night.

14. It seems that the Cubs will (loose, lose) another game.

15. The coach repeated, "Winners never (quiet, quit, quite)!"

LESSON 3

Decide on the Adjective or Adverb

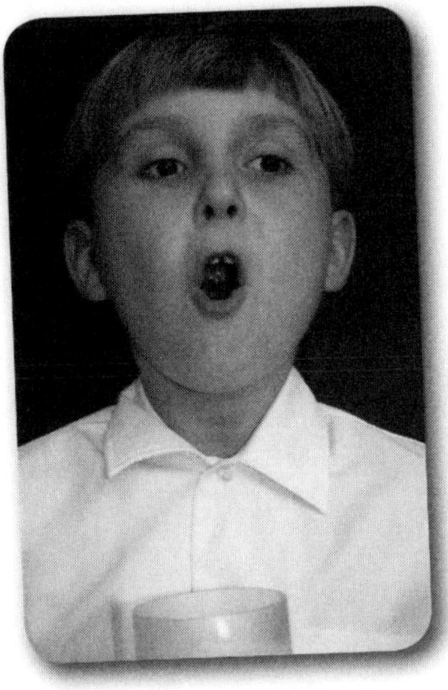

When deciding whether to use an adjective or an adverb, you must ask yourself, "What word am I modifying, or describing, in this sentence?"

An **adjective** modifies a noun or a pronoun.

The *sweet, clear* voices of the children rang out. (The noun *voices* is modified.)

I liked hearing their song. It was *soothing*. (The pronoun *it* is modified.)

An **adverb** modifies a verb, an adjective, or another adverb.

Tip

Adverbs are frequently formed by adding -ly to the adjective form.

careful → careful**ly**

The children sang *sweetly* and *clearly*. (The verb *sang* is modified.)

The song was *deeply* moving. (The adjective *moving* is modified.)

The children sang *extremely* sweetly. (The adverb *sweetly* is modified.)

The adjective *good* and the adverb *well* are often confused. *Good* is always an adjective, never an adverb. *Well* is usually an adverb.

***Good* modifies the noun *e-mail*. *Well* modifies the verb *writes*.**

I received another *good* e-mail from Jo. She writes so *well*.

Use an adjective after all forms of the linking verb *to be* (*am, is, are, was, were, been*) and after linking verbs such as *feel, seem, grow, taste, smell, look,* and *become*.

The solution seems *plain* to me. (not *plainly*)

Use *well* to discuss health.

Shenna looks *good* in purple. (not *well*)

Exception: Don't you feel *well* today?

Activity A **Circle the correct word in parentheses.**

1. The carpenter built the shelves (good, well).
2. He built (good, well) shelves.
3. Can you tell which word is used (correct, correctly)?
4. Nidia gazed (dreamy, dreamily) at the water.
5. The roller coaster dropped (sudden, suddenly).
6. The team played (bad, badly).
7. Everyone looked (frantic, frantically) for the missing jewels.
8. Tornadoes are (unusual, unusually) in this part of the country.
9. Please drive (careful, carefully).
10. Her smile is (beautiful, beautifully).

Activity B **Decide if the underlined adjective or adverb has been used correctly. If so, put a check mark on the line. If not, write the correct form.**

__________ 1. With her new eyeglasses, Maria saw the page <u>clear</u>.

__________ 2. The car sped <u>dangerous</u> close to the edge of the cliff.

__________ 3. The pitcher played <u>good</u> in the first two innings.

__________ 4. The animals growled and roared <u>hungrily</u>.

__________ 5. Josh's song does not sound as <u>well</u> as his others.

LESSON 4 Compare Correctly

Adjectives and adverbs can be used to compare two or more things. Make sure you use the correct form when you make comparisons. Ask yourself:

✔ Am I comparing two things or more than two?

✔ Should I add the ending *-er* or *-est* to the word, or should I use *more* or *most* with it?

If you are comparing two things, use the comparative form of the adjective or adverb.

The comparative form is made by adding the ending *-er* to all one-syllable words (young → younger) and many two-syllable words (early → earlier). For all three-syllable words and some two-syllable words, use the word *more* (muscular → more muscular, patient → more patient).

***Young*, *old*, and *big* are one-syllable words. *Muscular* and *rapidly* have three syllables.**

> Daniel is Pam's *younger* brother, but he looks *older*. He is *bigger* and *more muscular* than Raoul. He grew *more rapidly* this year than last.

If you are comparing more than two things, use the superlative form of the adjective or adverb.

The superlative form is made by adding the ending *-est* to all one-syllable words (big → biggest) and some two-syllable words (ugly → ugliest). Use the word *more* or *most* with longer adjectives (temperamental → most temperamental) and with adverbs that end with *-ly* (quickly → most quickly). Check a dictionary if you're not sure which form to use.

Of all the giants in the land, the *biggest, fiercest, ugliest,* and *most temperamental* of them all was Threetooth. He was also the giant who *most often* threatened the villagers.

When you make a comparison, add either an ending (*-er* or *-est*) or a word (*more* or *most*), but do not add both. Avoid "double comparisons."

Tip

When you add -er *or* -est *to a word, you may need to change the spelling. For spelling rules, see the Writer's Handbook.*

Wrong	Right
most funniest	funniest
more longer	longer
more dangerouser	more dangerous
most oftenest	most often

The words *good*, *well*, *bad*, and *badly* have irregular comparative and superlative forms.

Adjective/Adverb	Comparative	Superlative
good/well	better	best
bad/badly	worse	worst

Examples of Incorrect and Proper Uses

Wrong You did *gooder* than anyone else on the grammar test!

Wrong You did *more better* than anyone else on the grammar test!

Right You did *better* than anyone else on the grammar test!

Activity A **On each line, write the correct comparative or superlative form of the word in parentheses.**

1. Canada is the __________ country in the Western Hemisphere. (large)
2. "Please sing __________ this time than last time," said the chorus director. (energetically)
3. Today's weather looks __________ than the weather yesterday. (bad)
4. Caring for the environment is one of the __________ responsibilities we have today. (serious)
5. As time passed, Mr. Ryle grew __________ and meaner. (angry)

Activity B **In each sentence below, a modifier is underlined. If its form is correct, put a check mark on the line. If the form is incorrect, write the correction on the line.**

__________ 1. Of the four sisters, Rose has the <u>reddest</u> hair.

__________ 2. Marco is <u>more stronger</u> than his father.

__________ 3. This is the <u>most scary</u> movie I have ever seen.

__________ 4. Crows are <u>most intelligent</u> than parakeets.

__________ 5. Amanda's cold is getting <u>worser</u>.

Activity C **On a separate sheet of paper, write a paragraph in which you compare two people, places, or things. Use comparative and superlative forms of adjectives and/or adverbs in your comparison.**

Chapter 3

Writing Correct Sentences

A correct sentence is a group of words that expresses a complete thought. It includes a subject and verb. When sentences are clear and complete, the reader can move smoothly from one idea to the next.

LESSON 1 Fix Fragments

A sentence fragment is a group of words that does not express a complete thought. It is missing a subject, a predicate, or both. To turn a fragment into a complete sentence, add the missing part.

Tip

Use complete sentences in the writing you do for school and for the real world. Using incomplete sentences in a business letter, for example, would make you seem unprofessional.

A complete sentence has a subject and a predicate. The **subject** tells who or what the sentence is about and always has at least one noun or pronoun. The **predicate** tells what happens to the subject and always has at least one verb.

Subjects	Predicates
My *artwork* (noun)	*won* (verb) first prize.
Nicole (noun)	*called* (verb) the coach.
He (pronoun)	*whispered.* (verb)
The small *dog* (noun)	*was* (verb) full of energy.

To fix a fragment, identify the missing part and then add it to make the sentence complete.

Add a missing subject

Fragment Have heard of the ovenbird?

Complete Sentence Have you heard of the ovenbird?

Fragment Got its name from the kind of nest it builds.

Complete Sentence The ovenbird of South America got its name from the kind of nest it builds.

Add a missing predicate

Fragment The nest of hardened mud.

Complete Sentence The nest of hardened mud is woven in the shape of an oven.

Fragment The nest, which has a dome and is made of hardened mud.

Complete Sentence The nest, which has a dome and is made of hardened mud, resembles the bread ovens of the native peoples of South America.

Note that fragments may be shorter or longer than complete sentences.

Short complete sentences

Please visit us. Will you come? We can't wait!

Long Fragment Since you will be traveling across the country at the end of the summer, when you are near our home.

Complete Sentence Since you will be traveling across the country at the end of the summer, we hope you'll stop to visit when you are near our home.

Activity A

Label each word group below as either a sentence (*S*) or a fragment (*F*). On the lines, correct two of the fragments you identified.

____ **1.** The girl watched.

____ **2.** In a secret tunnel behind the wall.

____ **3.** Surprised everyone!

____ **4.** Come to my party.

____ **5.** The members of her family?

____ **6.** You will never leave me alone with that dog again!

____ **7.** Went to the store.

____ **8.** Because of the freezing temperatures.

____ **9.** Hoping for a great summer.

____ **10.** Three friends from the same neighborhood.

____

____

____

____

____

____

____

Activity B **Fix each fragment below. Write the complete sentence on the line.**

1. The maple tree on Elm Street.

____

2. Has to rake up all the leaves?

____

3. Mr. Jackson's mustache.

____

4. Because she loves animals.

____

5. Washed his face and brushed his teeth.

____

6. Although Maya didn't like hiking.

____

7. To the top of the tower.

____

8. Sprinted across the finish line.

____

9. The brand-new car.

____

10. Had to pay the shop owner for the broken clock.

____

LESSON 2 

Fix Run-on Sentences

Run-on sentences are two or more sentences that are run together incorrectly. Fix a run-on sentence by turning it into one or more complete sentences.

The run-on sentence below contains two sentences that are not separated by proper punctuation. For more about complete sentences, see Lesson 1.

> The game of tennis has many rules the main object is to hit the ball over the net so that your opponent can't hit it back.

Ways to Fix a Run-on Sentence

1. Separate it into two or more sentences.
2. Turn it into a compound sentence.
3. Separate the complete thoughts using a semicolon.

To turn a run-on sentence into two sentences. . .

✔ Place an end punctuation mark—a period, a question mark, or an exclamation point—after the first complete sentence.

✔ Place a capital letter at the beginning of the second complete sentence.

> The game of tennis has many rules. The main object is to hit the ball over the net so that your opponent can't hit it back.

You can also fix a run-on sentence by turning it into a **compound sentence.** A compound sentence is one that contains two complete sentences joined by a conjunction, such as *and, but, or, for, nor, yet,* or *so.*

To turn a run-on sentence into a compound sentence. . .

✔ Insert a comma after the first complete sentence. Then add a conjunction just before the second complete sentence.

The conjunction *but* is used to make a compound sentence.

> The game of tennis has many rules, but the main object is to hit the ball over the net so that your opponent can't hit it back.

✔ Add a semicolon between the two complete sentences.

Tip

When choosing how to correct a run-on sentence, ask yourself which method will best express what you want to say.

> The game of tennis has many rules; the main object is to hit the ball over the net so that your opponent can't hit it back.

Sometimes a run-on sentence incorrectly connects two complete sentences with a comma.

Incorrect Connection

> A tennis court is rectangular, its surface is generally clay or grass.

Possible Revisions

> **Two Sentences** A tennis court is rectangular. Its surface is generally clay or grass.
>
> **Compound Sentence** A tennis court is rectangular, and its surface is generally clay or grass.
>
> **Semicolon** A tennis court is rectangular; its surface is generally clay or grass.

Activity **Label each word group below as either a sentence *(S)* or a run-on sentence *(R)*. On a separate sheet of paper, fix all run-on sentences.**

____ **1.** The main character in this story dreams of becoming a doctor but cannot afford to go to college.

____ **2.** Representative Phil Bard became interested in politics when he was young at the age of eleven, he made campaign posters.

____ **3.** People often think that bats are harmful, these flying mammals help human beings in many ways.

____ **4.** For many Caribbean nations, tourism is the major industry, tourists are attracted to the warmth and beauty of these islands.

____ **5.** Some people go running on indoor tracks for exercise I like being outdoors.

____ **6.** Sentence fragments are common in spoken language and in ads, but students should make their sentences complete.

____ **7.** The snow melted on the mountaintops, as a result, the small town was flooded.

____ **8.** It snowed all morning and late into the afternoon, that night my brother and I made a snow fort, and all our friends came over to play in it.

____ **9.** I knew it would take a lot of work, but I decided to plant my own vegetable patch because I love making fresh salads and salsa.

____ **10.** Letitia just started learning Spanish this year, she is doing very well and can already ask for directions in almost perfect Spanish.

LESSON 3

Make Subjects and Verbs Agree

Your verb must always agree with your subject in number.

When you write about something that is happening now or happens regularly, you use verbs in the **present tense.** Note the present-tense verbs below.

Our dog, Rascal, *likes* music. If a song *comes* on the radio, he *starts* his act. First, he *dances* around the room. Then, he *whines*. After that, he *howls*. At that point, someone *turns* off the radio.

Tip

The ending -s appears on most singular verbs. If the subject is I or you, you don't need to add an ending to the present-tense verb.

Use a **singular verb** with a **singular subject.** A singular subject names one person, place, or thing.

Singular Subject	Singular Verb
He	*runs.*
Sam	*runs.*
The dog	*runs.*

A **plural verb** agrees with a plural subject, which names more than one person, place, or thing, such as *we, they,* or *the Jacksons.*

Plural Subject	Plural Verb
We	*run.*
They	*run.*
Sheryl and Lee	*run.*

Note the present-tense plural verbs that are italicized in these sentences.

> Rascal and Tops, our two dogs, *like* music. If songs *come* on the radio, they *start* their act. First, they *dance* around the room. Then they *whine.* After that, they *howl.* At that point, I *turn* off the radio.

The verb *be* has special forms in the present tense:

Singular	**Plural**
I *am*	we *are*
you *are*	you *are*
he, she, it *is*	they *are*
(singular noun) *is*	(plural noun) *are*

Tech Tip

If your computer has a "grammar check" feature, it will probably point out instances where your subject and verb do not agree. Though this feature is a helpful tool, do not rely on it. Always recheck your work yourself.

Be careful with the verbs *have* and *do.* When the subject is singular, the present-tense forms are *has* or *does:*

Plural Both cities *have* two high schools.

Singular The city *has* two high schools.

Plural Lisa and Juan always *do* a good job.

Singular He always *does* a good job.

Remember that the verb must agree with its subject, even if there are other words separating them.

singular subject — *singular verb*

The *building* with the two chimneys *is* the oldest in town.

In a sentence that is a question, the subject usually follows the verb.

> *plural verb* *plural subject*
> What *are* three *countries* in North America?

To find the subject in a sentence that is a question, turn the question into a statement. Then look for the subject and verb.

> *Three countries in North America are…*

Activity **Read each sentence. Circle the verb in parentheses that agrees with the subject.**

1. The museums on Bledsoe Avenue (contains, contain) interesting exhibits.

2. Celia and her sister Teresa (loves, love) wading in the creeks during the hot summer.

3. Even though the rest of his family is afraid of heights, Trevor (likes, like) rock climbing.

4. People all over the world (has, have) special holidays.

5. Two characters from Greek mythology, Daedalus and his son Icarus, (tries, try) to fly on homemade wings.

6. I always (enjoys, enjoy) reading funny stories.

7. Our teacher, Mr. Natti, (wears, wear) a suit and tie.

8. What (is, are) the difference between a hurricane and a tornado?

9. When my sister picks me up from school, we always (takes, take) the scenic route home.

10. I really (like, likes) thunderstorms.

LESSON 4

Use the Right Verb Form

The three most common forms, or principal parts, are present, past, and past participle. Regular verbs follow specific rules to form the past and past participle. Irregular verbs form them in ways that aren't predictable.

Tip

The verb be has special forms in the past.

Singular	Plural
I *was*	we *were*
you *were*	you *were*
he, she, it *was*	they *were*
(singular noun) *was*	(plural noun) *were*

Present	Past	Past Participle (Use with *has, had,* or *have.*)
Dogs *bark.*	Dogs *barked.*	Dogs (had) barked.
They *smile.*	They *smiled.*	They (had) smiled.
You *try* hard.	You *tried* hard.	You (had) tried hard.

The **present** shows an action happening now. The **past** shows an action that already happened. The past of a **regular verb** has a *-d* or *-ed* ending.

To form the **past participle** of a regular verb, add *-d* or *-ed*. Use a helping verb (*has*, *have*, or *had*).

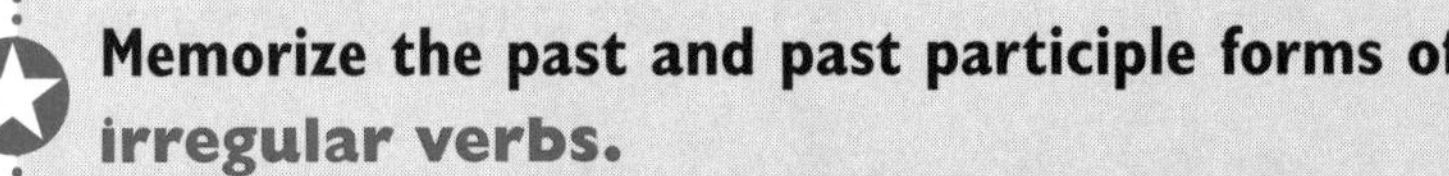

Memorize the past and past participle forms of irregular verbs.

Irregular verbs do not form the past and past participle by adding a *-d* or *-ed*. The following chart shows a sampling of commonly used irregular verb forms.

Tip

The fourth principal part of a verb is called the present participle. *For both regular and irregular verbs, the present participle is always the present form plus* -ing.

walk → walking
find → finding

Present	Past	Past Participle (Use with *has, had,* or *have.*)
be (am, are, is)	was, were	been
begin	began	begun
break	broke	broken
bring	brought	brought
catch	caught	caught
choose	chose	chosen
come	came	come
do (do, does)	did	done
eat	ate	eaten
find	found	found
fly	flew	flown
get	got	gotten or got
give	gave	given
go	went	gone
have (have, has)	had	had
know	knew	known
lead	led	led
mistake	mistook	mistaken
pay	paid	paid
ring	rang	rung
rise	rose	risen
see	saw	seen
take	took	taken
throw	threw	thrown
wear	wore	worn
write	wrote	written

Activity **In each sentence below, an incorrect form of the verb has been used. Rewrite the sentence using the correct verb form.**

1. I never seen such an amazing sight before!

2. The birds was in their nests.

3. Have you did your chores?

4. When the curtain rised, the audience became silent.

5. You written me an interesting e-mail.

6. With a high leap, Alonzo catched the fly ball.

7. The teacher waited quietly until the students taken their seats.

8. The figurine fell to the floor and broken into three pieces.

9. The friends had knew each other since they were four.

10. What has Luis brang to the party?

Chapter 4

Shaping Sentences

Careful writers try to make their sentences sound appealing because readers appreciate sentences that are varied, lively, and to the point. When you write, listen to the sounds of your sentences. Shape them to create natural, pleasing rhythms.

LESSON 1 Avoid Choppiness

Combine choppy, repetitive sentences to create more appealing sentences.

Read the following sentences aloud. Note how boring and repetitive they sound.

> I have read *Number the Stars* by Lois Lowry. I have also read *Dear Mr. Henshaw* by Beverly Cleary. I have read *The Whipping Boy* by Sid Fleischman.

Tip

When you combine sentences using and, but, *or* or, *add a comma before the word.*

I bought a book, and I read it the same day.

One way to reduce choppiness is to combine ideas, which will help you delete repeated words.

1. Use the word *and* to bring together related ideas:

> I have read *Number the Stars* by Lois Lowry, *Dear Mr. Henshaw* by Beverly Cleary, and *The Whipping Boy* by Sid Fleischman.

2. To combine ideas that show a contrast or difference, use the word *but*:

> **Choppy** Jerome read thirty-four books. He liked these three best.
>
> **Combined** Jerome read thirty-four books, but he liked these three best.

3. The words *who*, *when*, *which*, and *that* are also helpful when you are trying to combine choppy sentences:

Choppy Each book won the John Newbery Medal. The John Newbery Medal is a prize for the best children's book by an American.

Note the comma before *which*.

Combined Each book won the John Newbery Medal, *which* is a prize for the best children's book by an American.

Choppy A Newbery book has a gold medallion on it. The medallion tells about the award.

Use *that* to refer to things.

Combined A Newbery book has a gold medallion on it *that* tells about the award.

Choppy John Newbery was a British bookseller. He lived in the 1700s.

Use *who* to refer to people.

Combined John Newbery was a British bookseller *who* lived in the 1700s.

4. You can repair choppiness in other ways, too. Experiment with your sentences. Change word order, and vary the way your sentences begin.

Choppy One Newbery winner is *Adam of the Road*. It was written by Elizabeth Gray. It won the Newbery Medal in 1943. The story takes place in long-ago England. It is an exciting adventure story.

Combined Elizabeth Gray wrote the Newbery winner *Adam of the Road* in 1943. It is an exciting adventure story that takes place in long-ago England.

Activity A **Write a different revision of the "choppy" problem sentences in example 4 above. You may use two sentences.**

____

____

Activity B **Revise each of the groups of sentences. Combine ideas, delete words, add words, and change word order as you wish. Aim for sentences that sound more interesting and less choppy.**

1. Thanksgiving is a good time for family gatherings. Labor Day weekend also brings many families together. So do Fourth of July celebrations.

____

____

2. Rudy is on a basketball team. He has a pair of lucky socks. He wears the socks for every game. He never washes them.

____

____

3. Eduardo's parents immigrated to the United States. They came from El Salvador. They came in 2009. El Salvador is a country in Central America.

____

____

4. This morning I woke up. I brushed my teeth. I ate breakfast. I waited for the bus.

____

5. My uncle lives in Iowa. His wife and his children, Angela and Troy, live with him. They live on a farm. They grow corn. They also grow soybeans.

____

____

Activity C **Select a paragraph that you have recently written. On a separate sheet of paper, revise it, combining choppy sentences to create more appealing sentences.**

LESSON 2

Avoid Wordiness

Write concise sentences that are clear and appealing to readers. Avoid wordiness, which uses unnecessary words that can sound awkward and confusing.

Concise sentences come right to the point. To make your sentences concise, cut out repeated words and words that don't add anything to your meaning.

The writer crossed out unnecessary words.

Wordy Thomas Alva Edison was an American ~~who was born in the United States, and he was an~~ inventor who ~~invented things and he~~ held the world record of 1,093 patents.

Concise Thomas Alva Edison was an American inventor who held the world record of 1,093 patents.

Wordy His ~~well-known~~ laboratory was famous. It was ~~located~~ in Menlo Park, New Jersey. It was ~~in that place~~ where he invented the phonograph. It recorded ~~sounds~~ and replayed sounds ~~back so people could hear them again~~.

Concise It was at his famous laboratory in Menlo Park, New Jersey, that he invented the phonograph. It recorded and replayed sounds.

Activity

Look for unnecessary words in the following sentences. On the lines, revise the sentences to give the same meaning in a concise way.

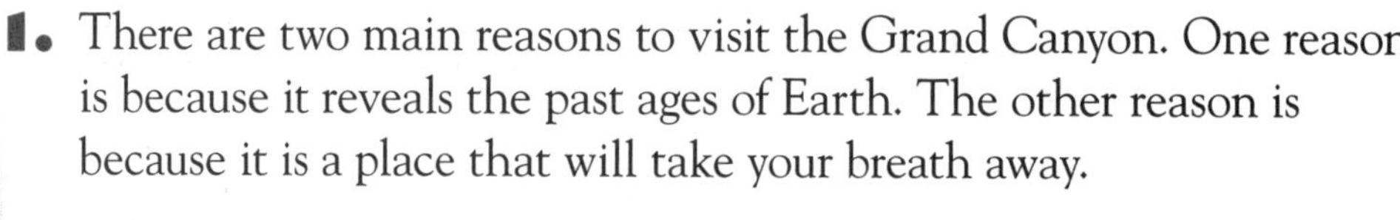

1. There are two main reasons to visit the Grand Canyon. One reason is because it reveals the past ages of Earth. The other reason is because it is a place that will take your breath away.

____

____

____

Activity *continued*

2. One invention that changed humankind was the wheel, and another influential invention was the printing press, and a third invention that changed history was the automobile. Today, the invention that is changing the world right now is the computer.

____

____

____

3. At one point in time millions of years ago, the separate continents of modern times were not separate. All the continents were combined in one supercontinent, and scientists have named that supercontinent Pangaea.

____

____

____

4. In the book *Nothing But the Truth* by Avi, the main character is a student whose name is Philip Malloy. One word that I could use to describe Philip Malloy is the word *foolish*.

____

____

____

LESSON  Use Sentence Variety

Varying the structure of your sentences makes your writing more interesting to read.

Although they are grammatically correct, these sentences are boring to read because most are the same length and begin the same way.

> Yesterday was Sunday. I went to the grocery store. I biked there. The store was closed. I went home. I read a book.

Tech Tip

When writing at a computer, if you want to check if your sentences are varied, save your current draft. Then, in a new document, cut and paste your sentences so that each appears as its own paragraph. Are they all around the same length? Do they all look similar? If so, edit to add variety.

Use a variety of sentence structures by. . .

1. writing different types of sentences
2. making your sentences different lengths
3. starting sentences in different ways

The sentences you read above are all **simple sentences.** They are made up of one independent clause. An **independent clause** is a group of words that contains a subject and a predicate and expresses a complete thought. It can stand on its own as a sentence.

Independent Clauses

> *subject* *predicate*
> *Yesterday* **was** Sunday.
>
> *subject* *predicate*
> *I* **went** to the grocery store.

A **subordinate clause** is a group of words that contains a subject and a predicate but doesn't express a complete thought. It cannot stand on its own as a sentence.

Subordinate Clauses

subject predicate If *I* **had** gone to the store on Saturday
subject predicate Because *I* **waited** until Sunday
subject predicate that *I* **biked** to

To make sentences more varied, you might create a **compound sentence.** It is made up of two or more independent clauses. One way to join two independent clauses is by placing a comma after the first clause and a conjunction (*and*, *or*, *for*, *nor*, *yet*, or *but*) before the second clause.

Compound Sentences

independent clause *independent clause* *Yesterday was Sunday*, and *I went to the grocery store.*
independent clause *independent clause* *I wanted to stay*, but *I went home.*

You could also make a **complex sentence,** which is made up of one independent clause and one or more subordinate clauses. In the second example, the subordinate clause is inserted in the middle of the independent clause.

Complex Sentences

subordinate clause *independent clause* *Because it was closed,* **I went home.**
subject *subordinate clause* *predicate* The **store,** *which is on Grove Street,* **was** closed.

As you vary the types of sentences you use, vary the length of your sentences as well. In the following paragraph, the writer uses both short and long sentences.

Yesterday was Sunday. I had to go to the grocery store because I had promised my mother that I would pick up something for dinner. I put on my helmet and biked through my neighborhood to the nearest grocery store. I saw that the lights were all off and the door was locked. I knew that the store was closed, so I went home.

Varying how you begin your sentences will also make your writing more interesting to read.

You can begin a sentence with. . .

- a subject
- a phrase
- a subordinate clause

Similar Sentence Beginnings

Yesterday was Sunday. I went to the grocery store. I biked there. The store was closed. I went home. I read a book. I fell asleep. The phone rang. It was my mother. I told her I hadn't gotten dinner.

Varied Sentence Beginnings

The italicized sentence beginnings are phrases.

On Sunday, I went to the grocery store. I rode my bike there. I saw that it was closed, so I went home. *Sitting at home,* I read a book. *In the middle of a sentence,* I fell asleep. Then the phone rang. It was my mother. Ashamed, I had to admit I hadn't gotten dinner.

Activity A

Combine each set of sentences to create varied sentences. You may use more than one sentence. There is no one correct response.

1. Camping is fun. The wilderness can be dangerous. Sudden storms come up. People get lost. Be careful.

2. Everyone says riding a bike is easy. I can't ride a bike. I tried to learn. I broke my arm. I don't bike.

Activity A *continued*

3. Mythology is interesting. It tells stories of gods, humans, and nature. Lots of myths have magic in them. They explain why things are the way they are.

4. Koalas are marsupials. They live in trees. The trees are in Australia. They only eat eucalyptus leaves. Koalas were once hunted for their fur. They almost became extinct.

5. Venice is a city in Italy. It contains many islands. The islands are in Venice Lagoon. It is known for its canals. The canals are like streets made of water. Many people use boats to get around Venice. The most famous kind of boat is the gondola.

Activity B

Rewrite each of the sentences below to vary the sentence beginnings. You may have to add details.

1. Jorge crept in the door.

   ____

2. My mother made me clean up the broken dish.

   ____

3. We all dressed nicely for dinner.

   ____

4. Delilah and Lawrence hurried to class.

   ____

5. We were feeling guilty, so we replaced Mrs. Chang's vase.

   ____

Activity C

Now write a paragraph of your own that describes a memorable day you have had. Make sure your sentences are varied.

Chapter 5

Building a Paragraph

When you write to explain or to persuade, you build with blocks of thought called paragraphs. A paragraph is a group of sentences that focuses on one main idea. Each time a new paragraph begins, it tells the reader to get ready for a new main idea.

LESSON 1 Write a Topic Sentence

Beginning each new paragraph with a topic sentence prepares the reader for the main idea of the paragraph. It also helps keep the reader *and* the writer focused.

When you are writing to give information (to persuade or to explain rather than to tell a story), start each new paragraph with a topic sentence. A **topic sentence** tells the reader what the paragraph is about.

A good topic sentence. . .

- ✔ identifies the subject of the paragraph
- ✔ sets up the point the writer wants to make about the subject
- ✔ interests the reader so that he or she wants to read further

Topic Sentence

This states the main idea of the paragraph—Caesar's unusual qualities.

Our neighbor's dog, Caesar, has some unusual qualities.

Another Topic Sentence

No one knows when the first baseball or football game was played, but we know exactly when and where the first basketball game was played.

Activity A **Circle the letter of the topic sentence that would best begin the paragraph. Then explain why you made your choice.**

1. People may be willing to pay for your creative, custom-made valentines, for example. Or you might have just the right sense of responsibility to walk and feed a dog when its owner is away. If you don't mind noise, you and a partner could offer your services to help direct activities at children's birthday parties. Business ideas are everywhere.

a. Everyone knows that kids can open a lemonade stand, but there are lots of other jobs you can do to earn money.
b. Starting a business can be interesting.
c. You'll need a sense of responsibility if you want to earn money.

____

____

____

2. Rosa Parks worked as a seamstress in Montgomery, Alabama. On December 1, 1955, she boarded a city bus to go home. She took a seat in the rear—the section she always sat in—the one marked for "colored passengers only." The bus filled up, and soon a few white people were standing without seats. City law required Mrs. Parks to give up her seat for a white person. She politely but firmly refused. She was arrested. Her case led to the famous Montgomery bus boycott, a major event of the civil rights movement.

a. One woman made a difference.
b. All over the world, people have fought for their civil rights.
c. One day in 1955, a woman on a bus changed American history.

____

____

____

____

Activity B **Decide what main idea each group of sentences below supports or develops. Then, on the lines, write a topic sentence that could introduce the paragraph. (Write a complete sentence, not just a title or a phrase.)**

1. Topic Sentence: ______________________________

____

A story in a book can be more absorbing than one on TV because with a book, you're using your imagination to form pictures. You can find a book on just about any subject, but the subjects on TV are limited to whatever the programmers decide to offer. Most important, when you are reading a book, you are not constantly interrupted by annoying commercials.

2. Topic Sentence: ______________________________

____

It's called the oldest continuously inhabited city in the United States. The Acoma people probably built their homes here nearly one thousand years ago. Their descendants still come to the pueblo for ceremonies and other gatherings, and a few families live here year-round. The pueblo of Acoma is also called Sky City. The name fits because Acoma sits on top of a sandstone mesa 357 feet above the New Mexican valley.

Activity C **Now, write a paragraph of your own on a separate sheet of paper. Make sure it has a clear topic sentence. Exchange paragraphs with a peer and ask if your topic sentence is clear and interesting.**

LESSON 2 Unify Your Paragraph

Every sentence in your paragraph should relate to your topic sentence and support your main idea. Remove any sentences that do not support the topic sentence.

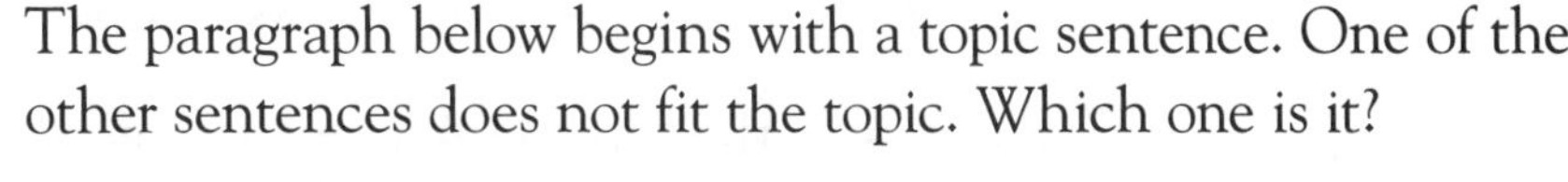

The paragraph below begins with a topic sentence. One of the other sentences does not fit the topic. Which one is it?

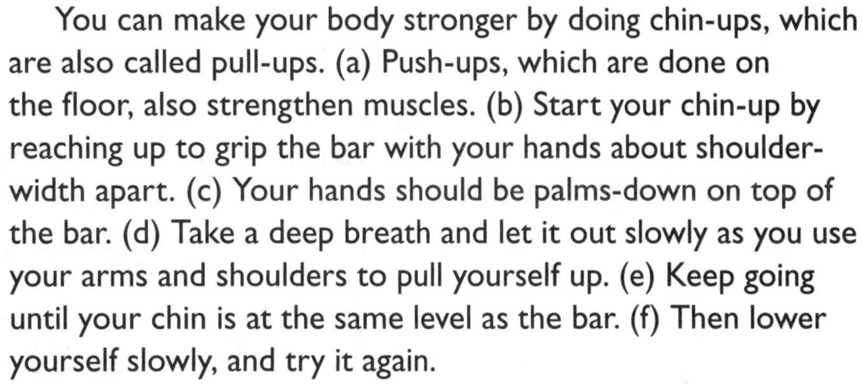

You can make your body stronger by doing chin-ups, which are also called pull-ups. (a) Push-ups, which are done on the floor, also strengthen muscles. (b) Start your chin-up by reaching up to grip the bar with your hands about shoulder-width apart. (c) Your hands should be palms-down on top of the bar. (d) Take a deep breath and let it out slowly as you use your arms and shoulders to pull yourself up. (e) Keep going until your chin is at the same level as the bar. (f) Then lower yourself slowly, and try it again.

If you said that sentence (a) was off the topic, you were right. The rest of the paragraph is about how to do a chin-up. A sentence about a different exercise—push-ups—does not belong in the paragraph.

Another way to unify your paragraph is to break it up into more than one paragraph.

As you revise your writing, ask yourself, "Do I have more than one paragraph here?" If your answer is yes, then use the proofreader's symbol ¶ to show where the new paragraph should start. As you read the following example paragraph, think about why the symbol belongs where it is shown.

Tech Tip

When writing on a computer using a word processing program, make sure you use a font that's easy to read.

> The main character in the story "I See You" is Mimi, a twelve-year-old girl who is terribly shy. When the story starts, she gets in trouble at school because she is too embarrassed to speak in class. She eats alone in the corner of the school cafeteria. Her only friend is her next-door neighbor's son, who is eight years old. ¶ Mimi has wishes and dreams, even though she never tells them to anyone. She loves to draw. She has a trunk full of portraits. She hopes to take art lessons someday.

Look back to the topic sentence. Do you see how it prepares the reader for details about Mimi's shyness? When the topic changes—to Mimi's wishes and dreams—a new paragraph is needed.

Activity A

Each paragraph below begins with a topic sentence. One of the other sentences does not support the topic. On the lines, write the letter of the sentence that should be deleted, and give a brief reason for your choice.

1. The members of our class have some outstanding skills and talents. (a) Eliza McCarthy has danced in the ballet *The Nutcracker* three years in a row. (b) Eliza's brother, who is two years younger, has also performed in the ballet. (c) Our classmate Eddie Perez won first prize in a photography contest. (d) Four of us represented our school in the Sports Day relay race, and our team came in first!

   Delete sentence ________ **because** ____________________________

   ____

2. The sunset was spectacular. (a) The sun swelled like a giant glowing balloon. (b) As it dipped into the ocean, pink and orange streamers seemed to fly out around it. (c) The ocean birds flew noisily nearby. (d) Then the orange glow vanished, and purples of every shade spread over the sky.

   Delete sentence ________ **because** ____________________________

   ____

Activity B **Each paragraph below should really be two paragraphs. Use the proofreader's symbol ¶ to show where the second paragraph should begin. Write a brief reason on a separate sheet of paper.**

1. Birds have remarkable eyesight. A golden eagle, for example, can detect a speck of motion one thousand feet below it. It dives and, in a flash, grabs the lizard or rabbit. An owl also has extraordinary vision. It is a night hunter, and its enormous eyes help it see in the dark. Other animals are known for their amazing hearing ability. Bats, for example, find their way around in pitch-black caves by using sound waves. Dolphins use sound waves to detect objects underwater.

2. To make yourself a great student, get organized! Set aside an uncluttered study area for doing homework. Get a separate folder for each subject and after-school activity. Get an assignment notebook to keep track of daily and long-term assignments. Map out a day-by-day schedule that includes time for homework and activities. Once you've set up a plan, follow it. Check off each daily assignment after you do it. Break long-term assignments into smaller parts, and tackle one part at a time.

3. My older brother is the greatest! He taught me how to fish, and every weekend during the summer, we go to a pond and fish together. He also threw me a surprise party for my birthday this year. He invited all my friends to it and had all my favorite foods there. Sometimes he gets mad at me, though, if I interrupt while he's studying or practicing on the violin. He takes his responsibilities very seriously. I have to remember that even though he'd like to be hanging out with me, he can't always.

4. I have always been a strong leader. In second grade, I organized a Camping Club that met weekly. I would arrange for wilderness experts to come to our meetings and teach us the skills needed to camp. I was chosen to be the captain of the softball team, which I have led to many wins. If I were elected Student Body President, I would make positive changes in the school. I would put recycling bins in every classroom. I would plan charity events such as food drives and dance marathons.

LESSON 3 Give Enough Support

When you write to persuade or to inform, you need to support your ideas with different kinds of supporting details, such as facts and information.

Supporting your ideas will. . .

- ✔ help readers understand your writing
- ✔ strengthen your points
- ✔ show that you are a trustworthy source of information

First Draft

One of my favorite exhibits at the Museum of Science is the Soundstair. It looks just like a regular set of steps, but it makes music. I like to walk, jump, and run up and down the steps.

The writer of that paragraph should give the reader more information about the Soundstair. What is it exactly? How does it work? What does it sound like?

Revised Draft

At the Museum of Science, one of my favorite exhibits is the Soundstair. It looks just like a regular set of steps, but it makes music. An invisible light beam shoots across each step. When someone's foot breaks through the light beam, a signal goes to a computer-controlled musical synthesizer. Instantly, there is a musical tone that sounds like a xylophone or even a bird. I like to walk, jump, and run up and down the steps. The speed and rhythm of my footwork create all sorts of musical patterns.

When you are revising your paragraphs, ask yourself, "Do I need to tell more?" If so, you should **elaborate,** or explain in greater detail.

Details to Add

✔ **facts:** things that can be proven true
✔ **examples:** things that illustrate a point
✔ **reasons:** causes or explanations why something occurred
✔ **statistics:** specific numbers, such as amounts or percentages
✔ **dates:** specific times when events occurred

Activity A **Each paragraph below contains a topic sentence and two supporting details. On the lines, come up with a third supporting detail. Try to add a kind of detail that isn't used in the paragraph.**

1. Everyone can play a part in taking care of Earth and its resources. People can drive to work together instead of alone so that they save fuel and cause less pollution. By turning off their faucets and not allowing water to run needlessly, people can conserve water.

____

____

2. This winter's weather has been especially harsh. The first snowstorm began on October 15 and lasted two days. There have been twenty days when the temperature has dropped below zero degrees Fahrenheit.

____

____

Activity B **On a separate sheet of paper, write a paragraph about your favorite place. Include at least two details about your chosen place. Make sure you give your reader enough information about the place.**

Chapter 6

Organizing Ideas in a Paragraph

As you have learned, a paragraph develops and supports one main idea. To best support that idea, organize your paragraph logically, and use transitions to connect ideas and sentences. Depending on your purpose, you may organize your supporting details in a variety of ways.

LESSON 1

Use Patterns of Organization

In a paragraph, organize your details in a way that fits your writing purpose. Three patterns are chronological, order of importance, and cause and effect.

To choose the pattern of organization that best fits your paragraph, ask yourself the following questions.

- ✔ What is my purpose in writing?
- ✔ What does my reader need to know to understand my paragraph?
- ✔ At what point in the paragraph does my reader need to be introduced to the details he or she needs to know?

If you are describing a series of events, such as in a story or how-to essay, you might use **chronological order,** also called time order.

Words that Signal Chronological Order

first, second, next, later, then, yesterday, at six o'clock

If you are writing to persuade or inform, such as in a speech or research paper, try using **order of importance.** State your most important reasons or details first and your least important ones last, or state your least important details first and your most important last.

Words that Signal Order of Importance

most important, least important, primarily

You might use **cause-and-effect** order to organize a paragraph that persuades the reader to take action about a problem. In cause-and-effect order, you state a cause and then discuss the effects it produces.

Words that Signal Cause-and-Effect Order

because, due to the fact that, as a result

As a writer, you can choose many ways to structure a paragraph. Experiment with different kinds of structures to see which one works best for the information you are presenting to your reader.

Activity A

The sentences in the paragraph below are out of order. On a separate sheet of paper, rewrite the paragraph with the sentences reordered. Use one pattern of organization, and explain your choice.

I should go on the school trip to Italy. (a) Most important, it would be a valuable life experience I would always remember. (b) In Italy, I could try lots of different foods. (c) I would get much better at speaking Italian. (d) I would also get to see famous works of art in person. (e) Furthermore, it would teach me to be responsible for myself.

Activity B

On a separate sheet of paper, write your own paragraph using one of the patterns of organization described in this lesson.

LESSON 2 Use Transitions

To connect your ideas and help your reader follow the order of your thoughts, you need to use transitions. Transitions are words and phrases that connect one sentence or idea to the next.

Planet Earth is tilted as it travels around the Sun. The Sun hits the northern and southern halves of Earth at different angles. North America has winter. The northern half of Earth is tilted away from the Sun. South America has summer. The southern half of Earth is tilted toward the Sun.

The writer of that paragraph needs to connect ideas better. Note how the transition words in the revised paragraph below make the paragraph's meaning clearer.

Cause-effect transitions

Example transition

Order of events transitions

Planet Earth is tilted as it travels around the Sun. As a result, the Sun's rays hit the northern and southern halves of Earth at different angles. For example, North America has winter when the northern half of Earth is tilted away from the Sun. At the same time, South America has summer because the southern half of Earth is tilted toward the Sun.

Transition words. . .

- ✔ show clear connections between ideas in sentences
- ✔ help your reader understand how one idea is related to another by showing contrast, cause-and-effect, or the order in which events happened
- ✔ help you add ideas or give examples
- ✔ make your sentences read more smoothly

Commonly Used Transition Words and Phrases

Tip

To choose a transition, ask yourself, "How do these two sentences relate to each other?"

To Give Examples	To Show an Added Idea	To Show a Contrast
for example	and	although
for instance	also	but
in fact	in addition	however
such as	besides	different from
	too	on the other hand
To Show Causes and Effects	**To Show Time**	
as a result	first	
because	then	
since	finally	
therefore	later	

Activity **Use transition words to make clearer connections between each pair of sentences below. You may combine sentences. Write your revisions on a separate sheet of paper.**

1. On Saturday, Mr. Virva played golf in the morning and softball in the afternoon. He showed up for league night at the bowling alley.

2. Dogs love attention and will do almost anything to get it. Cats have too much pride to beg.

3. Max ate six slices of pizza and three hot dogs. He woke up at midnight with a stomachache.

4. Katarina is a fabulous swimmer, a great soccer player, and a top student. She is a good friend.

5. Eddie's family speaks Spanish as its first language. He needs to study for Spanish class.

LESSON 3

Write a Description

When you write a description, you should include specific sensory details to create clear and detailed images in your reader's mind. You should also use a pattern of organization, such as spatial order.

A descriptive paragraph puts your reader "right there" with the person, animal, place, or object you are describing.

Sample Descriptive Paragraph

Sensory details

Specific details

Spatial order

I gaze at the scene. Branches filled with dark green leaves form an upper curtain. Looking beyond them, I see a sunlit field. Tall grass, yellow and green, stands quietly. Wildflowers—pink, purple, blue, and every shade of red—are spattered everywhere. No breeze, no birds' songs, no buzzing insects disturb the restful silence. In the distance, just along the curving line where the meadow meets the piercing blue sky, is a tiny figure. The person appears to be sitting alone and looking at the scene, just as I am. Does the person see me watching? I have never found out, though I have stared at this scene countless times as it hangs on a wall of our living room.

Tip

In the sample paragraph, the transitions upper, beyond, in the distance, along, *and* where *tell the reader where to look next.*

The diagram below shows the order of this paragraph.

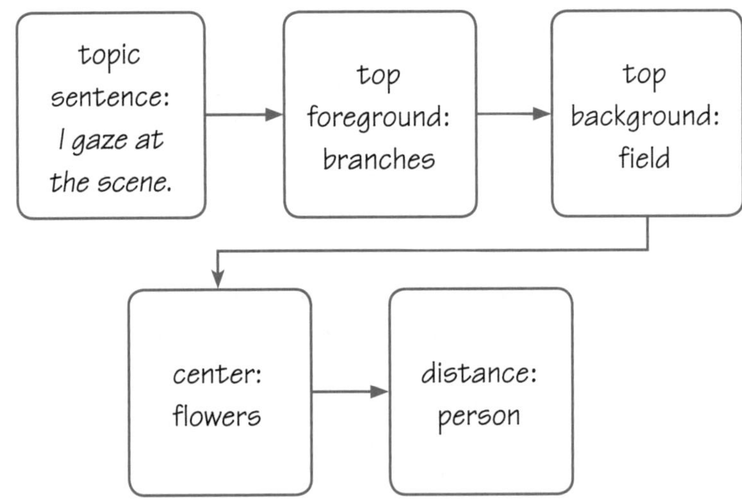

Tech Tip

If you want, you can put a picture in your writing. Under the "Insert" menu, choose "Picture" and add your picture.

The writer has used **spatial order,** the order in which things are located in space, to lead the reader through the scene.

Some Transitions that Signal Spatial Order

top	to the left	below
in back of	beside	surrounding

A descriptive paragraph should also include **sensory details** that appeal to the senses. In the example paragraph, sensory details help the reader see the colors, hear the silence, and feel the restfulness of the scene. Use sensory details that appeal to all of your reader's senses.

The Five Senses

Sense	Sample Details
Sight	A parrot, red and yellow, flashed through the trees.
Hearing	The steady drip of the leaky faucet kept me awake all night.
Touch	My horse's nose is softer than velvet.
Taste	I picked a blackberry from the bush and crushed it until its tart juice trickled on my tongue.
Smell	The neighbors could always tell when Nana made her chicken soup.

In the pairs of sentences below, the second sentence of each pair has a stronger effect on the senses. When you write a description, sharpen it with exact details that include sensory words.

Vague The mosquitoes bothered the picnickers.

Better The picnickers slapped frantically at the mosquitoes, whose high-pitched whines rose and fell like sirens.

Vague I did not like the look of that meatloaf.

Better My tongue turned suddenly dry as I noticed that grayish blobs seemed to be growing on the meatloaf.

Activity A **Each sentence below could be made more vivid with sensory details. On a separate sheet of paper, write a more descriptive revision of each sentence.**

1. I like swimming.
2. It is nice to stay at the cabin by the lake.
3. The Fifth Street Deli has good sandwiches.
4. The skyscraper is tall.
5. The room was messy.

Activity B **Each numbered item below features a main idea of a descriptive paragraph. On a separate sheet of paper, write three supporting sentences for each. Use descriptive details that will put your reader "right there."**

1. The house looked as if no one had lived in it for years.
2. The weather changed suddenly.
3. Main Street is filled with activity.
4. Toni has an interesting sense of style.
5. I stared at the dessert.

Activity C **On a separate sheet of paper, write a descriptive paragraph about this picture. If you like, you can write an acrostic poem. Each line of the poem begins with one of the letters of the word *tiger.* You can also write a different kind of poem. It does not have to rhyme or have any particular form.**

Writing a How-to Essay

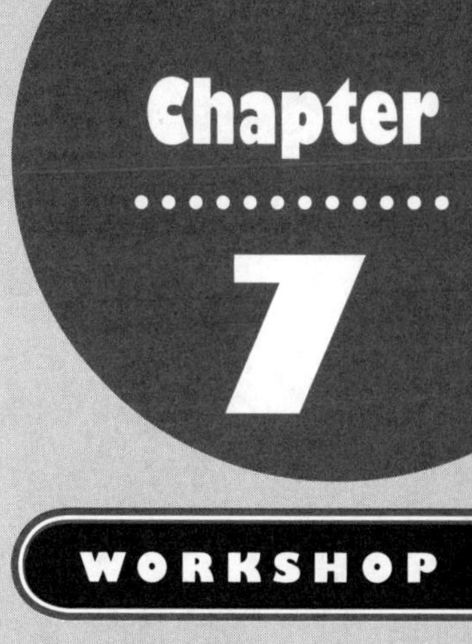

An essay is a piece of nonfiction writing that focuses on a single topic. Essays can serve many different purposes. In the following chapter, you will learn to write a how-to essay. A how-to essay explains, step by step, how to complete a specific task, such as making a recipe, fixing a bike chain, or planting a garden.

WORKSHOP

LESSON 1 Develop Ideas

Before beginning to write, you must choose the topic of your essay. You must also determine your essay's thesis, or main idea, and make a plan.

First, you must choose a topic. Use one of these methods:

1. Freewrite. Focus on a single word, such as *ocean,* and let your ideas flow freely.
2. Brainstorm. Use a web diagram like the one below to brainstorm a list of possible topics

When you use a web, put a broad subject in the middle. Then, in the outer circles, list narrower topics that fit under the category of that broad subject.

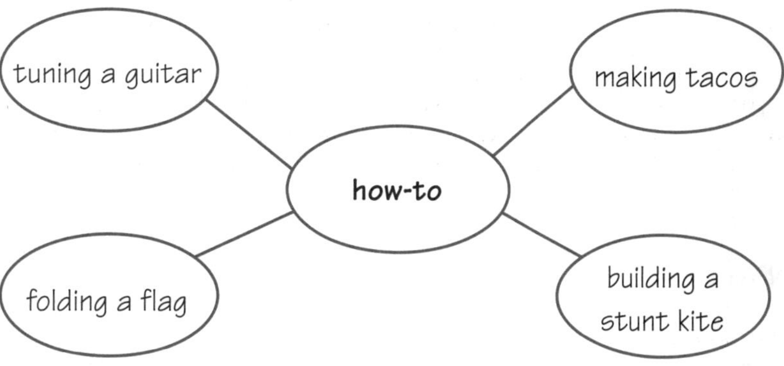

The task you choose should. . .

✔ be something you know how to do well
✔ interest you
✔ be something you can successfully explain to readers

You must also decide what **thesis,** or main idea, you will develop in your essay. Your thesis should not be too broad or too narrow. It should also state why the task would interest the audience.

Too Broad Building a kite is really cool.

Too Specific Most kites are made from nylon.

Just Right Kite-making is an exciting hobby that is easier than you might think.

Next, list the steps involved in the process. Use a graphic organizer, such as the one below, to jot down each step. Do the following.

✔ Begin by listing all of the materials your audience will need.
✔ List the steps in the order they should be done.
✔ Use transition words, such as *first, next, then,* and *while.*

Tip

Making an outline can be very helpful. Make sure you have an introduction; the body, which lists all of the steps and the materials needed; and a conclusion, which restates your thesis and leaves readers with a feeling of completeness.

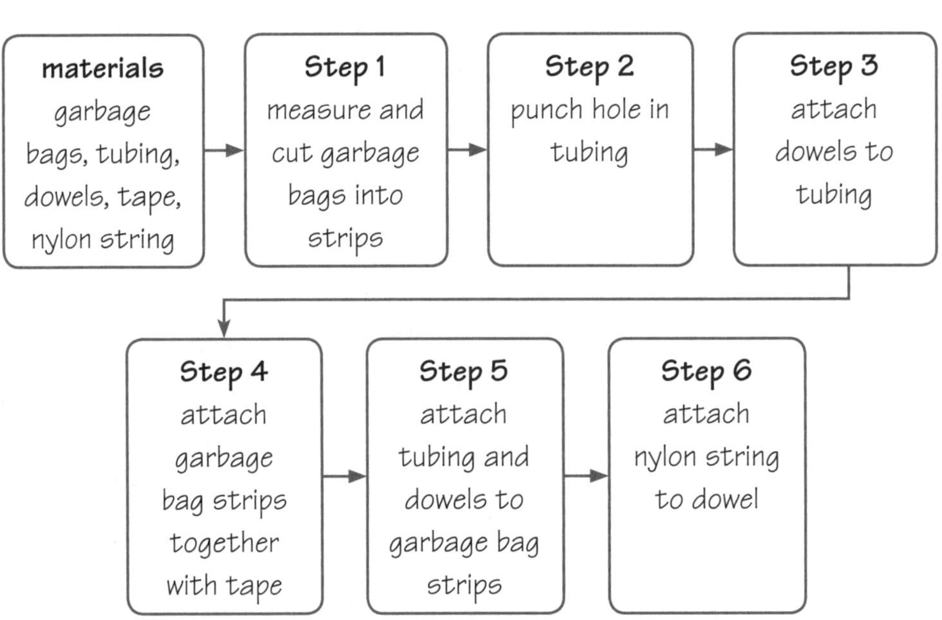

Because you've done the task many times, it's easy to forget small steps. Review your organizer to make sure you listed every step.

Activity A

Use the web below to brainstorm possible topics for your own how-to essay. Add more circles if necessary.

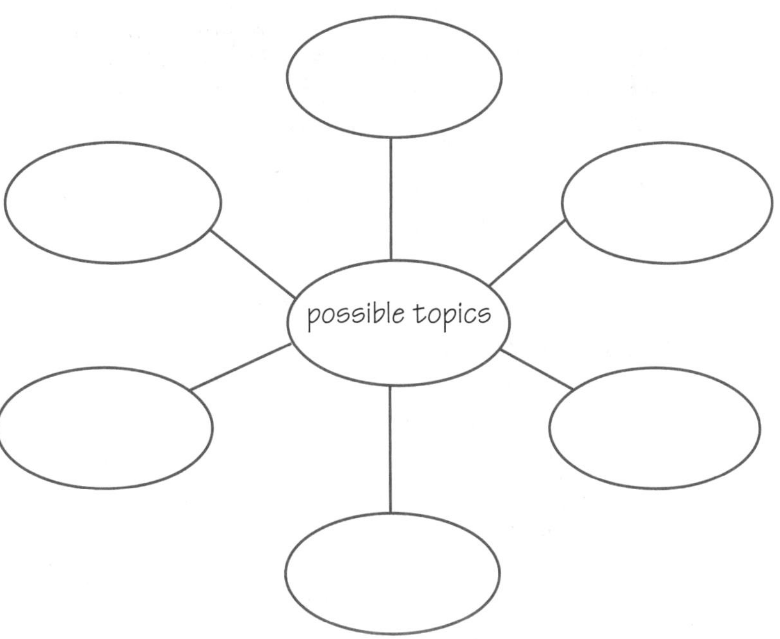

Activity B

Choose one of the topics you listed in the web above. Then write the thesis you will develop in your essay. Make process notes below. Use the example as a model. Use as many boxes as necessary.

Thesis: ____

____

materials → Step 1 → Step 2 → Step 3

Step 4 → Step 5 → Step 6

LESSON 2

Write an Introduction

All strong essays begin with an introduction. The introduction is the reader's entrance into the essay.

A good introductory paragraph. . .

✔ introduces readers to the topic and thesis of the essay
✔ grabs the attention of readers
✔ makes readers want to read more

In the previous lesson, you saw the example thesis for a how-to essay: "Kite-making is an exciting hobby that is easier than you might think." Here is an introduction that presents that major idea:

Tip

As in this sample, the last sentence of the introductory paragraph is often the best place to state the major idea, or thesis.

> Have you ever wanted to reach up and touch the sky? You might be surprised to learn that with a few strong sticks, a roll of string, and a large garbage bag, it *is* possible to touch the sky. With these everyday objects, you can build a simple kite that can soar hundreds of feet off the ground. Kite-making is an exciting and rewarding hobby that is easier than you might think.

This introduction is effective because the reader wants to continue reading to find out how easy and exciting kite-making is. The essay's body should answer the questions raised in the introduction. You can use the methods below to make an exciting introduction.

At the beginning. . .

1. add a vivid description
2. state an interesting fact
3. ask a question

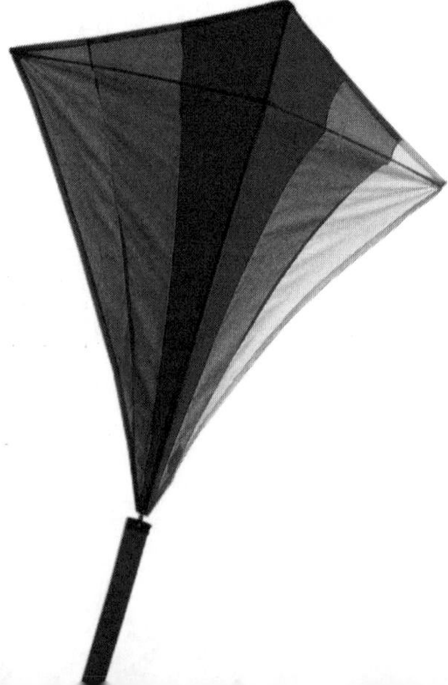

Activity A Read the essay introduction below, and answer the question that follows it.

Are you tired of going to movies you don't like just because you can't think of anything else to do? Well, there's a way to both keep yourself entertained and make the type of movie you'd like to see. All you have to do is think of a movie you'd like to see and make it yourself. With a friend or two, a video camera, and some creativity, you can make a movie of your very own.

What thesis will the writer develop in the body of the essay?

____

____

____

Activity B Look back to Activity B in Lesson 1. Find the plan you made for your how-to essay based on the topic you chose. Use the lines below to write a first draft of an introduction that presents that thesis.

____

____

____

____

____

____

Activity C With a peer, take turns reading the drafts of your introductions aloud. Tell your partner what you liked about his or her introduction. Give helpful, respectful advice about what you think he or she should do in a revision. Then revise your introductory paragraph, keeping your partner's advice in mind.

LESSON 

Explain the Process

The purpose of a how-to essay is to explain a process, a series of steps that leads to a result. In the body of your essay, you will explain the process of completing your task.

Tip

A topic sentence tells the reader what the main idea of the paragraph is. Make sure that every sentence in each body paragraph relates to the paragraph's topic sentence.

Successful body paragraphs include. . .

✔ **Topic Sentences:** Each body paragraph should focus on a single topic and begin with a topic sentence.

✔ **Materials:** After the topic sentence in your first body paragraph, give a list of all of the materials your readers will need to complete the process.

✔ **Chronological Order:** Describe each step in the process in the order in which that step should be performed.

Your reader may need special equipment, ingredients, or materials to complete a process. The best place to tell the reader about necessary materials is at the start of the first body paragraph, right after the topic sentence:

> Before getting started on your kite, you will need to gather your materials. These materials include a 13-gallon garbage bag, eight 36-inch hardwood dowels, eight pieces of vinyl tubing, two garbage bag ties, packing tape, a spool of nylon string, scissors, and a ruler. After gathering these materials, you are ready to build your kite.

Use words and phrases that signal time order so that your reader knows the correct order in which to perform each task. Examples of these transitions include *first, next, after that, when, while, until, then, finally,* and *at last.*

Refer to your process notes to guide you in writing your paragraphs. You should cover no more than two or three steps in a single body paragraph.

Example of a Process Paragraph

Time-order words are highlighted.

A ride on a roller coaster can be a thrilling experience, especially if you know how to get the most out of it. The first step, called anticipation, occurs while you are waiting in line. Listen carefully as people around you describe their most horrible, life-threatening experiences on roller coasters. When your heart starts pounding with fear, you're ready to move on. The next step is selecting a seat; if possible, head for the front or the rear (the middle is less scary).

After you are seated, grip the bar in front of you as tightly as you can until you lose all feeling in your fingers. While the car slowly climbs to the highest point, whimper like a terrified puppy. At the moment you reach the top and see the sharp drop below, let out an ear-piercing scream. After that, just keep screaming. Finally, the ride will come to a stop. At that point, you can say, "Let's go on again!"

Activity **Refer to the introductory paragraph you wrote in Activity B of Lesson 2. Now write two or three body paragraphs to follow that introduction. Include a topic sentence for each body paragraph and a list of materials.**

____

____

____

____

____

____

LESSON 4 Write a Conclusion

An essay should come to a satisfying close. An effective conclusion makes readers think again about the writer's thesis. In a how-to essay, the conclusion should state the end result of the process and tell the reader what to do with it.

Tips for Writing a Conclusion

- ✔ suggest how your reader should use the end product
- ✔ restate your thesis
- ✔ emphasize why the task or product is special or important
- ✔ give your reader a sense of completeness
- ✔ leave the reader thinking about your essay

Does not restate the thesis or suggest how to use the product

Then you're done. You might not want to make a kite. Some people don't like it. But if you do want to, this is how to make one.

Strong Concluding Paragraph

Restates the thesis

While it takes patience and a little bit of hard work, you too can build a kite that's ready to take to the skies. Without a doubt, kite-making is a fun hobby that just might surprise you.

Activity **Write the first draft of an effective conclusion to your essay. Refer to the rough outline you made in Activity B of Lesson 1.**

WORKSHOP

Writing Model

An excellent how-to essay. . .

- ✔ includes an introductory paragraph that grabs readers' attention and introduces them to the topic and major idea
- ✔ is organized chronologically and includes signal words
- ✔ clearly explains what materials are required
- ✔ concludes by briefly restating the major idea in a new way
- ✔ maintains reader interest throughout with precise language and fresh, original ideas

Below is the final version of a how-to essay.

The essay opens with a question that grabs reader attention. The major idea, or thesis, is in the last sentence.

Making a Kite

Have you ever wanted to reach up and touch the sky? You might be surprised to learn that with a few strong sticks, a roll of string, and a large garbage bag, it *is* possible to touch the sky. With these everyday objects, you can build a simple kite that can soar hundreds of feet off the ground. Kite-making is an exciting and rewarding hobby that is easier than you might think.

The topic sentence focuses attention on materials. The signal words *Before getting started* tell the reader that a process begins here.

Before getting started on your first simple kite, you will need to gather your materials. These include a 13-gallon garbage bag, two 24-inch-long, ¼-inch-diameter hardwood dowels (round sticks), a big spool of string, and scissors. You might also want to invite a friend to help, especially one who likes to tie knots. After gathering these materials, you are ready to build your kite.

Begin by arranging the wooden dowels so that one crosses the other. You want the intersection to be about three-quarters of the way up the vertical dowel and halfway across the horizontal dowel.

The writer uses spatial and chronological signal words to keep instructions in order.

Use string to tightly lash the two dowels together where they cross. When that knot is tight, attach a three-foot piece of string to the same location. Let it hang free for now.

continued

Next spread out the garbage bag. Position your dowels on top of the garbage bag. Neatly cut the garbage bag into a diamond shape to connect to the dowels. Attach the bag to each dowel end with more string. Just wrap the string around the dowel and the loose tip of the bag over and over until you have a tight coil. Make a knot so the coil won't come undone.

The writer answers questions a reader might ask, such as, "What about that loose piece of string?"

Now take that loose piece of string from the middle. Poke a hole through the plastic about halfway along each side of the horizontal dowel. You will have two holes total. Run the string through one hole, across the outside of the plastic, and in through the other hole. Tie its loose end to the end that is already tied where the dowels cross (see the paragraph that begins "Use string"). You will have a loose loop called a bridle. Pull the loop toward you, and where it tightens against your hand, tie on the free end of your spool of string. This is your flying line. Finally, go outside and start running in the wind to fly your kite!

The conclusion restates the thesis in a new way.

While it takes patience and a little bit of hard work, you too can build a kite that's ready to take to the skies. Without a doubt, kite-making is a fun hobby that is easy to learn. In no time at all, you can fly a masterpiece of your own design.

Assignment

Now write your own how-to essay. Choose a topic, draft an attention-getting introduction, and use chronological order for your body paragraphs. Wrap it all up with a conclusion that restates your thesis.

Writing an Autobiographical Incident

WORKSHOP

A narrative may be a paragraph long or a thousand pages long; it may be true or fictional, funny or sad. However, all narratives are stories. They convey, or communicate, an experience. In this lesson, you will learn how to write a short narrative called an autobiographical incident.

LESSON 1 Analyze a Model

An autobiographical incident describes an important event in the writer's life. Autobiographical incidents show how the event made a major impact on the writer's life.

Autobiographical incidents. . .

- ✔ focus on one short event in the author's life
- ✔ are usually brief
- ✔ include specific descriptions of the event, the people involved, and the writer's feelings
- ✔ include sensory details, or details that appeal to the five senses (sight, touch, taste, sound, and smell)
- ✔ include dialogue, or conversations, to bring the story to life
- ✔ are organized in chronological order, with transitions such as *first, next, then, moments later, until that time*, and *soon afterward*

Read the following autobiographical incident. As you read it, note the features from the checklist above that the writer used.

Tip

When you include dialogue, remember to use quotation marks. Begin a new paragraph each time a speaker changes.

Terry is one of my oldest friends. We have known each other since we were in the first grade. Around the Fourth of July, Terry told me that some kids in her neighborhood were going to throw a party. "Great," I thought, "finally, some excitement." Up until that point, the summer had been about as much fun as a broken Slinky®. The party was scheduled for the following weekend, so Terry and I got together to choose our outfits.

"This is going to be my first unsupervised party," Terry said while rummaging through her closet.

"What do you mean?" I asked.

"No parents. It's just us kids," she said as she pulled out a big purple hat. My stomach sank like a bowling ball. I knew my mom and dad would never go for it. I couldn't lie to them, but I didn't want Terry to think I was a wimp. What could I do?

The speaker describes her feelings.

The night of the party finally came. I was all dressed up and sitting anxiously in my room. I knew my mom was going to ask me whose parents were supervising the party. "How can I lie to her?" I thought. I knew I couldn't do it. It was wrong. I called Terry's house and told her I couldn't go. She started to laugh and said: "I'd rather spend the night with you than go to some lame party anyway."

Sensory details

I couldn't believe what a good friend Terry turned out to be. We ended up on my back porch most of the night, drinking extra-sweet lemonade and watching fireworks fill up the sky like flowers.

Activity **Answer the questions below.**

1. Write a summary of the autobiographical incident.

____

____

____

____

____

2. What point is the narrator illustrating?

____

____

____

3. How effective is the model? Explain why.

____

____

____

4. What is one suggestion you would make to improve the model?

____

____

____

LESSON 

Choose an Experience to Convey

Brainstorm a list of incidents from your life, and choose the most suitable one to convey in your autobiographical incident.

A good incident to write about. . .

- ✔ is brief
- ✔ illustrates a point
- ✔ is a detailed memory (you remember clearly what happened and who was involved)
- ✔ can be told in an interesting and/or entertaining way

The writer began with broad categories and narrowed them down to specific memories.

Brainstorming a list of all the possible topics that come to mind can help you find the best topic for your autobiographical incident. Below are two Thinking Trees filled with possible topics for an incident about a personal experience.

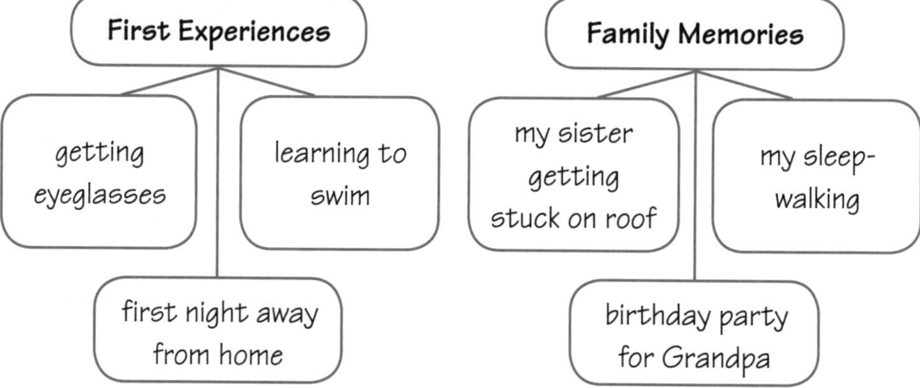

Save the list of topics you have brainstormed in your writer's notebook. A certain memory might not be right for this assignment, but you might want to use it later as a topic for something else, like a poem or a short story.

Activity A **Fill in the Thinking Tree with your own list of possible incidents. Start with a broad category, such as "Vacation" or "Sports." Then list specific incidents related to that category. You can make more Thinking Trees on a separate sheet of paper.**

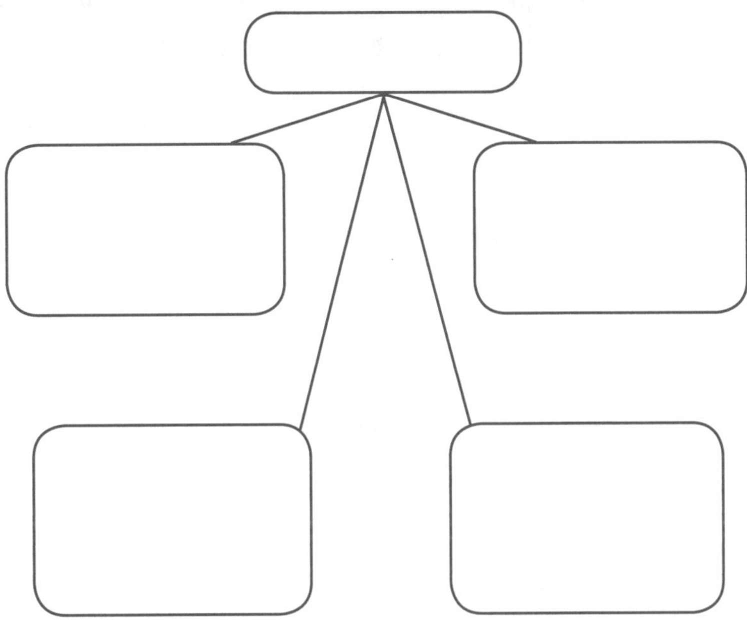

Activity B **Think about the list you generated. Using the checklist on the previous page, choose the experience that will make the best topic for an autobiographical incident.**

1. My autobiographical incident will be about. . .

____

____

2. The main reason that topic is a good one is. . .

____

____

LESSON  Think About the Reader

To make sure your audience has the knowledge it needs to understand your autobiographical incident, give necessary background information. Also, clearly state what the incident meant to you.

Even though you know all about the experience you're describing, you have to remember that your reader might know nothing about it.

Let your reader know. . .

- ✔ what happened
- ✔ where and when it happened
- ✔ who was involved
- ✔ why the incident is worth recalling

Start your autobiographical incident by stating the point the incident illustrates. Capture the readers' attention.

> It's been said that "you can have too much of a good thing," and I believe it.

The rest of this autobiographical incident will tell what happened when the writer entered a pancake-eating contest.

> Sometimes a person just needs to get away from it all, and that's what I decided to do.

The rest of this autobiographical incident will tell about an incident that occurred when the writer was five years old and wandered away from his babysitter.

 **Make a plan for writing your autobiographical incident.**

Jot down notes you can refer to as you write. You can use them to make sure that you include all the information the audience needs to understand your story. Here, for example, are the writer's notes for the autobiographical incident you read in Lesson 1.

Tip

As you plan your autobiographical incident, think about how you'll show what the characters in the incident are like, perhaps through their actions and dialogue.

I. Finding out about the party
   a. boring summer
   b. Terry's neighbors throwing a party

II. Preparing for the party
   a. Terry is one of my oldest friends
   b. got outfits ready for the party
   c. Terry told me it would be unsupervised

III. Night of the party
   a. I didn't want Terry to think I was a wimp
   b. I knew I'd have to lie to my parents
   c. really anxious
   d. told Terry I couldn't go

IV. Instead of going
   a. Terry didn't mind; would rather be with me
   b. had fun sitting on my back porch

If you compare these notes to the final autobiographical incident, you will see that the writer made changes in their order and added more information. Notes are useful, but expect to make changes as you write.

Activity A **Craft a topic sentence for the incident you chose in the previous lesson. Make sure your topic sentence introduces the reader to the point of the autobiographical incident.**

Activity B **Make a plan for your autobiographical incident. Use the example plan above as a model. Look back at the checklist on the first page of this lesson to be sure you have included all the essential information.**

WORKSHOP

Writing Model

An excellent autobiographical incident. . .

- ✔ tells a true story about the author that illustrates a clear point
- ✔ includes all the information that a reader needs to understand the incident
- ✔ uses dialogue and transition words to help readers follow the sequence of events

Below is the final version of an autobiographical incident.

The phrase "used to" hints that the main point is about what changed between the writer and his brother.

The writer describes the setting and then uses dialogue to move the action along.

A Competition Goes Wrong

My younger brother Ned and I used to spend all our time competing. We competed about everything, from making the smartest chess moves to yelling the loudest to finishing a meal in record time. I won most of the time because I'm older, stronger, faster, and, usually, smarter. That just made Ned want to compete more. And that suited me just fine. I love winning.

One quiet Saturday morning, our parents were sleeping late and some old cartoons were on the television. My sisters were doing an art project at one end of the family room. Ned and I were sitting on the floor in our pajamas, watching cartoons and throwing a foam football. Inspired by the cartoons, we started to argue about which one of us would make the better cowboy.

"I can ride a fast horse," Ned bragged.

"I can rope a huge bull," I replied, and threw the football at Ned's stomach.

"Well, I can rope a bull and pull it over with my horse," Ned insisted, while tossing the football at my head.

"Oh yeah?" I said. "Well, I can rope you right now!"

I grabbed some plastic twine from a bunch of my mom's flower-arranging supplies and wrapped it around Ned's ankle. I tied a knot and pulled it really tight. Ned started yelling.

continued

My sisters started yelling at us to knock it off, but Ned was fast. He took the free end of the twine and wrapped it around my right arm. He tied a knot while I tried to get away.

The writer keeps the action moving with transition words and short sentences.

By now there was enough yelling to wake up my parents. Dad came stomping in. We all stopped moving and got quiet. He looked at Ned and me. We kept quiet. Who knew what would happen now?

Quietly, Dad started laughing. He tried to swallow it, but it popped out. He was still laughing when he said, "Okay, boys, let's go show Mom what you've been up to." He turned and started out of the room.

The writer says how the incident made him feel.

We couldn't walk. Ned could stand with the twine around his ankle, but I had to crawl with the other end around my arm. We started wrestling when we realized how silly we looked. I also kind of felt like crying. I was really mad at Ned for making me look like a loser. It's not exactly that he won—but neither did I.

Meanwhile, Dad and my sisters were crying, they were laughing so hard. Then Mom came in and said, "How lovely that you're all having such a nice time this morning!" That made everyone laugh even harder.

The concluding paragraph returns to the point the writer made in the introduction and states what the writer learned from this incident.

I won't forget that day for a long time. I didn't like being laughed at. Worse than that, though, was learning that Ned wasn't always slower or dumber than I am. From that day on, I usually stopped to think before daring Ned to compete with me.

Assignment

Now write your own autobiographical incident. Use your topic sentence and your outline as a guide, but keep looking for ways to improve your paper as you draft it. Be sure to tell how you feel about the incident and/or what you learned from it.

WORKSHOP

Writing a Persuasive Essay

During a disagreement, you've probably said to someone, "I just wish you'd see things my way!" You *can* show others how you see things using your writing. You can persuade readers to understand your viewpoint and to agree with it by expressing an opinion and supporting it with sound reasons and convincing examples.

Persuasive writing occurs in varied forms: essays, letters, reviews, and more. This lesson focuses on a short form, an opinion essay of one to three paragraphs.

LESSON 1 Open with a Thesis Statement

Start your persuasive essay by crafting a thesis statement that clearly states your opinion on the issue or subject and at least two reasons for your opinion.

An **opinion** is a statement of belief rather than a provable fact.

Fact	Opinion
Mr. Norman teaches four French classes.	Mr. Norman's French classes are exciting.
We camped at Lake Freedom last summer.	If you want a fascinating vacation, try camping at Lake Freedom.
The movie *Attackers* lasts two and a half hours.	You should avoid seeing the movie *Attackers*.

In your thesis statement, clearly state your opinion and at least two reasons for it. Make sure your thesis statement is neither too broad nor too narrow. Avoid simply stating a fact or identifying the topic.

Too Broad Many changes need to be made in our school.

Too Narrow Tutoring support should be available for two hours on Wednesdays.

Stating a Fact Some schools offer tutoring after school.

Identifying Topic My paper will be about school.

Revised By adding new after-school activities and tutoring support, we can improve our school.

Activity A **Below are two thesis statements for a persuasive essay. On a separate sheet of paper, explain which thesis statement is stronger. Revise the weak statement.**

1. There are many fun things to do over the summer, such as going to the movies, taking a vacation, or doing other activities.

2. Building a new park on Simpson Street is a bad idea because of the traffic on Simpson and the number of parks in that area.

Activity B **Prepare to write your own persuasive essay. Use the prompts below to generate a list of possible topics. Then choose the best topic. Write your thesis statement on a separate sheet of paper.**

A small action that would make a big difference. . .

It is unfair that. . .

One thing that I wish would change around here. . .

Tip

When choosing a topic, ask yourself:

- *How strongly do I feel about this?*
- *Can I convince readers to agree with me on this?*

LESSON 2 Develop Strong Support

The reasons you listed for your opinion must be supported by evidence. Use strong supporting details, such as facts, examples, and quotations, to convince readers of your argument.

Tip

Use a graphic organizer like this when gathering your evidence.

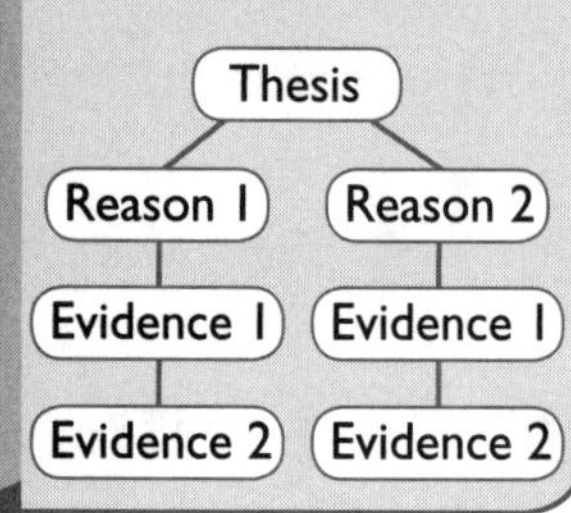

A student named Martin is writing an essay to support his opinion that students should raise money to help pay for field trips.

Thesis Statement Students should raise money to help pay for their own field trips because the school cannot afford to fund the trips and students are more than capable of raising the money.

Martin should use a variety of details to support his thesis statement. A **fact** is a statement that can be proven true. You may need to do research to find facts such as names, dates, and numbers.

Fact The school budget for field trips has been cut by 50 percent this year.

Examples are specific incidents.

Example With adult help, students at Lake Middle School successfully organized fund-raising activities, such as bake sales, car washes, and read-a-thons.

Quotations are the exact words of an expert on the topic.

Quotation Our principal has said, "Only one-fourth of the students were able to pay full field-trip fees last year."

Tip

Use only ***relevant*** *evidence, or evidence that actually relates to the topic you are discussing. Irrelevant statements, which are beside the point, weaken your argument.*

You should address counterarguments, which are arguments that someone might raise against your opinion.

Think about what someone might say to argue against you. What can you say to show that your opinion is stronger?

A Counterargument to Martin's Opinion

Students are in school to learn, not to earn money.

Martin's Response to the Counterargument

This contrast word signals that Martin is telling why that objection is not a strong one.

Some people might say that students should be spending their time learning instead of raising money. However, most of our fund-raising takes place after school and on weekends, not during school hours. In addition, the money raised makes possible all the learning that occurs during the field trips themselves.

Activity A

Read each thesis statement and the two lettered statements below it. Circle the letter of the statement that offers stronger support. Explain why the other statement is weaker.

1. Mr. Washington, our art teacher, should have his own classroom because he is a wonderful teacher and traveling from room to room disrupts students' learning.

   a. Art is an important and valuable subject that does not get enough attention.

   b. Students lose learning time because Mr. Washington must set up his equipment every time he comes to a classroom.

____

____

Activity A *continued*

2. Because of the hard work I put in and the opportunities I miss, I deserve to be paid for babysitting for my little brother.

a. Babysitting is hard work and should not be done free of charge.

b. Because I babysit for Albie every afternoon, I am not available to take babysitting jobs that would pay money.

____

____

3. My parents should allow me to join an organized baseball league because playing baseball would help me make friends and develop as a person.

a. Just about all the kids in town are on some kind of organized team.

b. Organized sports teach kids to practice a skill until they get better at it.

____

____

Activity B

Look at the thesis statement you wrote in Activity B of Lesson 1. Ask yourself, "What counterargument might someone who disagrees with me raise?" Write one or more sentences in which you state a counterargument and then tell why it is not strong. Remember to use a contrast word such as *however, but,* or *although*.

____

____

____

____

____

____

LESSON 3 Persuade Your Audience

Plan your persuasive essay by choosing which reasons and supporting evidence to use and the strongest order in which to present them. Finish your essay with a conclusion.

As you plan your persuasive essay. . .

- ✔ list your reasons
- ✔ list all your supporting evidence, including any counterarguments and the response you will use to counter them
- ✔ look over your list, and delete any weak evidence
- ✔ decide in what order you will present your evidence

Suppose that a student named Hilda would like to attend Hilltop Middle School instead of Valley Middle School. Below is the beginning of her plan for a short persuasive essay that she intends for her mother to read.

Thesis Statement I would like to attend Hilltop Middle School because it has better resources and more opportunities for me than Valley does.

Reason 1 Better resources at Hilltop.

~~**Evidence 1** More students at Hilltop than at Valley.~~

Evidence 2 Hilltop only school with up-to-date equipment in computer lab **(2)**

Evidence 3 Hilltop's building—newer, better condition **(1)**

Hilda deleted an irrelevant piece of evidence and renumbered the remaining evidence in the order in which she will present it. Writers often choose to save their strongest evidence for last, where it may have the most impact.

Hilda's Essay

Hilda devoted her first body paragraph to a counterargument and response.

Her second paragraph describes her supporting reasons.

> I would like to attend Hilltop Middle School. I know that I could walk to Valley Middle School instead, but distance is not a big problem. Although Hilltop is farther away, I could walk to the bus stop at Fletcher Avenue or get a ride with Marcia and her dad.
>
> Hilltop is the better school for me because it has better resources than Valley. The building is newer and in better condition. In addition, Hilltop has a lab with up-to-date computers. Valley has older computers that are often broken.
>
> Most important, Hilltop is the only school with a choral group, and I would like to try out for it. Hilltop also has a better selection of advanced-level courses, which would make me stand out on college applications.

Tech Tip

As you write, remember that spell-checkers are not perfect. Use them, but always proofread your work as well.

An essay needs a **conclusion,** a final reminder or convincing comment.

Your conclusion should. . .

- ✔ restate the opinion you present in the essay
- ✔ emphasize the importance of your opinion
- ✔ leave the reader thinking about your essay

> My heart is set on Hilltop, so I hope I will be there in the fall.

You also might have a whole concluding paragraph.

> Valley Middle School might seem like the most convenient school for me to attend. But in order for me to receive the best education possible, I need to attend a school that I care about. I would be excited to go to school at Hilltop every day because of its great resources and opportunities. Hilltop would offer me the best education, so it is the school I wish to attend.

Activity A

Below is a persuasive essay. As you read it, think about whether or not the writer has persuaded you. Name at least one thing that the writer has done well and at least one thing that needs to be improved.

I should be allowed to go to an overnight camp at Camp Miniwatha this summer. Although I have never spent more than a week away from home, it would be an important experience that would help me learn how to take care of myself.

All of my friends are going to be attending Camp Miniwatha. If I don't go with them, I'll be very lonely this summer. More importantly, I could learn many special skills by attending this camp. They have a stable where they give horseback riding lessons. I've always wanted to learn how to ride horseback, but I've never had the opportunity to. Miniwatha also has a great arts and crafts program, and I was thinking that I could use the skills I could learn there, like candle making or leatherworking, to make and sell crafts once I come back home.

Like I said before, I should be allowed to go to Camp Miniwatha this summer.

____

____

____

Activity B

Continue to plan your own persuasive essay. On a separate sheet of paper, make a plan using the sample from this lesson as a model. Be sure to list your reasons and evidence.

Activity C

Using the guidelines from this lesson, write a conclusion for your persuasive essay on a separate sheet of paper. Use the checklist on the previous page to help you craft it.

Activity D

Trade your plan and conclusion with a partner. Give helpful suggestions or reasons he or she might want to include or objections he or she might want to counter.

WORKSHOP

Writing Model

An excellent persuasive essay. . .

✔ opens with a clear thesis statement that shows the writer's opinion on the topic
✔ provides strong reasons and relevant evidence
✔ includes possible counterarguments and responses to them
✔ ends with a conclusion that restates the writer's opinion

Below is the final version of a persuasive essay.

The essay opens with a clear thesis statement that directly states what the essay will be about and outlines the main points.

The first paragraph focuses on one reason and supports it with evidence.

The second paragraph states and develops a second reason.

The Better Middle School

I would like to attend Hilltop Middle School because it has better resources and more opportunities for me than Valley Middle School does. At Hilltop, the facilities are newer, there is a greater range of extracurricular activities, and the students are more serious about their studies. Hilltop provides an all-around better education.

One reason that Hilltop is a better school is that the building is newer and in better condition. The computer lab has up-to-date equipment, while Valley has older computers that are often broken. I can learn new computer technology and use the skills both in and out of school. The Hilltop gym has a new pool and a track, which is important to me since I am interested in both swimming and running.

Hilltop is also the only school with a choir. I have not had the chance to be in choir. I think that given the opportunity, I would really enjoy it. I like to sing, and I would like to develop this skill further. I also have heard that the choir teacher is excellent and helps every student improve individually. The choir even traveled to Washington, D.C., last spring to sing at the White House!

The author uses clear references and statistics to support the thesis.

Most important, according to Uncle Rich, who has taught at both schools, the students are more serious about their work at Hilltop. I think being surrounded by students who are enthusiastic about learning and who complete their assignments on time would encourage me to do the same. I know that I am in middle school, but developing good habits now will help me in college. For example, the school brochure says that 85% of Hilltop graduates go to college, which is drastically higher than Valley's statistics. This statistic is most likely the result of a quality education beginning at a young age. For these reasons, I think I would work harder at Hilltop.

The author presents a counterargument and then responds to it.

I know that I could walk to Valley Middle School instead, but distance is not a big problem. Although Hilltop is farther away, I could walk to the bus stop at Fletcher Avenue or get a ride with Marcia and her dad. Also, the school provides a directory of students, so I could arrange a carpool with other students who live in my neighborhood. When it comes to good education, I don't think that distance should be taken into consideration.

The concluding paragraph sums up the essay by restating the thesis.

Hilltop Middle School is a much better place for me than Valley. The resources and facilities are much better, the activities are plentiful, and the students are serious about their schoolwork. In order to get the best education, it is important for me to go to the school with the most to offer. My heart is set on Hilltop, so I hope I will be there in the fall.

Assignment

Now write your own persuasive essay. Use your outline and notes to guide you, but make whatever changes are needed to improve your paper.

Chapter 10

WORKSHOP

Strategies for School Success

What does it take to be an outstanding student? Students who seem to know all the answers and consistently earn high grades are not necessarily smarter than average students. Nearly anyone can become a top student by making the effort to learn a few strategies for handling schoolwork and putting them into practice.

LESSON 1

Take Notes

Tip

When you write down essential information, you begin to fix that information in your memory. Putting information into your own words will help you understand it better.

Take notes to get the most out of what you read. Three ways of taking notes are writing down essential information, using graphic organizers, or making index cards.

Taking notes can help you understand textbook chapters, newspaper and magazine articles, charts, graphs, and online sources, such as Web pages. The method you use for taking notes depends on your purpose. Imagine you are preparing for a test. Read the text on the following page. Then reread it, jotting down **essential information** such as names, dates, and key points.

Note-taking Strategies

- Copy headings and jot down the important facts and ideas related to each.
- Look for numbers, dates, and place names.
- Look for phrases that signal major ideas.
- Use abbreviations and your own shorthand.
- Look for questions in the text itself, and write down your own answers.

Tech Tip

To find reliable sources, visit your local library's website. Try using its reference database to find newspaper and magazine articles.

The Pyramids of Giza

The ancient world was said to have "seven wonders." Only one of those wonders still stands—three immense stone pyramids near Cairo, Egypt. The pyramids, engineering marvels constructed over decades as tombs for three Egyptian kings, have stood for 4,500 years.

The Great Pyramid

Khufu was an Egyptian king of the Fourth Dynasty, which lasted from about 2575 B.C. to 2465 B.C. (A dynasty is a ruling family.) As king, Khufu was considered an earthly god. Egyptians also believed that the king would continue to live as a god after the death of his human body. To ensure the king's eternal status, complex rituals surrounded the preservation and burial of the body. Specialists dried and wrapped the body so that it would last forever as a mummy.

Khufu's monument is known as the Great Pyramid because it is the largest of the three pyramids at Giza. Its planning and construction lasted about 20 years and required tens of thousands of workers. It covers about 13 acres, is more than 40 stories high, and contains over 2 million stones, each weighing an average of 2 tons. The pyramid weighs 5,750,000 tons in all. Technical questions remain about how it was built using simple tools and bare hands.

Notes on the Passage

Pyramids of Giza 1

- only 1 left of "7 wonders" of ancient world
- near Cairo, Egypt
- 3 stone pyramids, tombs for 3 kings
- 4,500 yrs old

Abbreviations

Key terms and their definitions

Great Pyramid 2

- size
  - largest of 3
  - 13 acres, 40+ stories, 2 mil. stones, 2 tons each avg.
- built by King Khufu to ensure eternal role as god
- planning and bldg., 20 yrs, tens of thousands of workers
- still not known exactly how achieved

Terms

- dynasty—ruling family
- mummy—dried, wrapped, preserved body

Dates

- Fourth Dynasty (Khufu's): about 2575 B.C. to 2465 B.C.

You can also take notes in **graphic organizers.** Graphic organizers show information in a visual way. They also show how one piece of information relates, or connects, to another. See the organizers below.

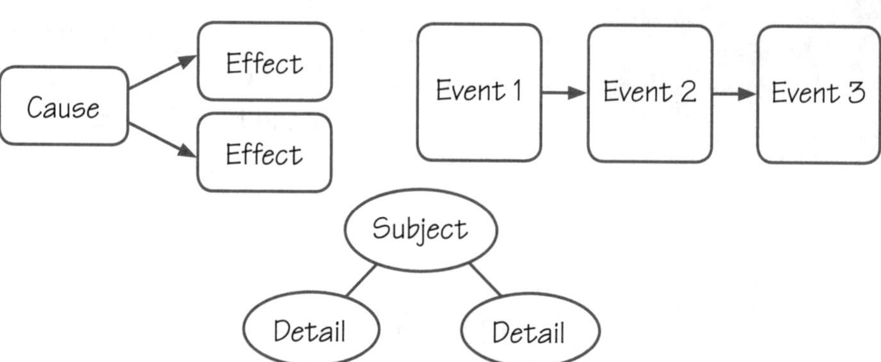

If you are writing a research paper, you want to gather accurate information from a variety of sources. Try using **index cards.**

When making index cards. . .

- ✔ write a question you want to answer at the top of each card
- ✔ write notes from the text that answer your question
- ✔ name the source of the information and the page on which you found it

Quotation marks show that the note-taker has copied exact words from the source.

What have X rays of Egyptian mummies shown? 3

- jaw & skull shapes show family relationships among rulers
- health
  - "... the most serious health problems arose from the environment, from the Nile and the desert."
  - Nile worms infected human body
  - avg. life span—35–40 yrs
  - sand in food→extreme tooth wear→infections, even death

Tales Mummies Tell, Patricia Lauber. NY: HarperCollins, 1985.
pp. 40–43, 46–47

If you are writing a report, you will need to provide a list of sources. As you research, use separate cards to list each of your sources. Number each source card. These samples show how to list sources using the MLA style of documentation.

Tip

If you use source cards, you do not have to list the full information about the source at the bottom of the card. Just add the number of your source card.

Book

Romer, John. The Great Pyramid: Ancient Egypt Revisited. Cambridge: Cambridge University Press, 2007. Print.

Magazine Article

Sapet, Kerrily. "Steps and Stones: Who Built the Pyramids?" Appleseeds 9.2 (Oct. 2006): 10. Print.

Encyclopedia Article (Online)

"Killer whale." Encyclopædia Britannica. 2008. Encyclopædia Britannica Online. Web. 28 April 2008. <http://www.britannica.com/eb/article-9045439>.

DVD or Film

A Life Among Whales. Dir. Bill Haney. DVD. Public Broadcasting Service, 2005.

Activity A **On a separate sheet of paper, take notes on the essential information from this passage.**

Baleen Whales

Most of the giant whales—humpback whales, gray whales, blue whales, and others—have **baleen** instead of teeth. Baleen, a material similar to the hooves of mammals, is arranged in brushlike plates in the upper jaw of the whale. The baleen serves as a filter in which the whale's food is caught. Baleen whales feed on tiny **crustaceans,** or shellfish. One common food source is **krill,** shrimplike crustaceans that are only about two inches in length. Baleen whales have developed a variety of feeding methods to trap huge numbers of krill in their bristly baleen.

Activity B **Answer the following questions about this note card on a separate sheet.**

What is group life like for killer whales? 3

- "The killer whale's social structure is highly evolved."
  - constant communication with underwater vocal sounds
- Typical herds have 25–30 members

Minasian, pp. 178–179

1. Why do quotation marks enclose the first sentence under the question?
2. What does "Minasian, pp. 178–179" mean at the bottom of the card?

Activity C **On a separate sheet of paper, write a bibliography entry for a book by James Cross Giblin titled *The Riddle of the Rosetta Stone: Key to Ancient Egypt*. It was published in 1993 by the New York publisher HarperTrophy.**

LESSON 2

Summarize

Summarizing is an effective study method in which you retell only the most important ideas of a text.

Summarizing is helpful if you are trying to learn and remember information. It is a way of checking your own understanding.

Tips for Writing a Summary

✔ Decide what the main idea is and begin your summary by stating it.

✔ Include only the details that are necessary to understand the main idea.

✔ Use your own words.

✔ Make your summary short. It should be no more than one-third of the length of the original text.

✔ Do not include your opinion.

The paragraphs below form a **plot summary,** which includes only the basic information about the setting, characters, conflict, and major events.

Tip

When you summarize fiction, only include the key details:

- *names of the main characters*
- *setting*
- *author's name*
- *title of work*
- *brief description of the plot*

In the English fairy tale "Jack and the Beanstalk," a poor widow sends her son Jack to sell their cow, but Jack exchanges the cow for a few beans instead. Jack's mother tosses the beans out the window, but the magic beans grow into an enormous beanstalk reaching to the clouds. Jack climbs the beanstalk to the land of a mighty giant. The giant's wife hides Jack from the giant, who wants to eat him.

Jack steals the giant's riches and escapes down the beanstalk. Jack and his mother are no longer poor, but Jack returns to the giant's land two more times to steal more riches. The final time, the giant chases Jack down the beanstalk. Jack chops down the beanstalk and the giant falls to his death. Jack and his mother are rich. Jack weds a princess and lives happily ever after.

Read the article below and the summaries that follow.

Tip

When you summarize nonfiction, only include:

- *author's name*
- *title of work*
- *main idea and key details that support it*

Leave out:

- *long explanations or quotations*
- *most examples*

If someone were asked to draw a picture of a whale, chances are that the drawing would show a creature with a long, thick body, with a blunt head at one end and two small flukes at the other. The drawing would resemble a sperm whale. Although people often picture a sperm whale when they think of a "typical" whale, the sperm whale has unique qualities.

The sperm whale is the largest of the toothed whales. The male, which is larger than the female, can grow to nearly 60 feet in length and weigh up to 53 tons. The sperm whale is not as large as the most enormous of the baleen whales (which do not have teeth), but the sperm whale does have the largest brain of all whales. Actually, it has the largest brain of any animal that has ever lived!

The sperm whale is also among the deepest divers of all whales. Like all mammals, it must breathe air. But it can remain underwater for an hour at a time, feeding more than 3,000 feet below the surface.

Sperm whales are hunters and chase after giant squid, their main food, in the ocean depths. Sperm whales have also been known to attack small boats. (The famous white whale of fiction, the furious Moby Dick, was a sperm whale.)

Strong Summary

Four paragraphs of information have been reduced to a three-sentence summary.

Though the sperm whale seems "typical," it has many unique traits. The sperm whale is the largest of the toothed whales, is one of the deepest divers of all whales, and has the largest brain of any animal. The sperm whale is also an aggressive hunter of giant squid and has attacked boats.

Weak Summary

This summary does not include the main idea of the text. The quotation is too long, and the writer includes too many examples.

> A sperm whale has a "long, thick body, with a blunt head at one end and two small flukes at the other." It can be 60 feet long and can weigh 53 tons, which is bigger than other whales that have teeth and not baleen. It can stay underwater for a long time, for an hour even. It eats squid. Squid live deep in the ocean. In the book Moby Dick, Moby Dick was a sperm whale.

Activity A **Write a summary of any story you have read. (You may need to reread the story.)**

____

____

____

____

Activity B **Read the informational passage. Then, write a summary of it in no more than four sentences.**

Sperm whales often form groups that scientists call nursery schools or nursing pods. These groups may have up to fifty members. Nursery schools are made of related female whales and their offspring—youngsters and newborn calves. The adult whales protect the younger whales, sometimes by banding together to fight off attacking sharks.

Male sperm whales are called bulls. Most of the time, they live separately from the females. Full-size bulls, which are at least 20 years old, often are seen traveling alone. Younger bulls live together in "bachelor pods," migrating together to feed in cold northern waters.

____

____

____

LESSON 3

Prepare a Research Paper

In this lesson, you will learn how to write a research paper. A research paper presents details from a variety of reliable sources to explain a single topic to readers.

> **Tip**
>
> *In a research paper, be formal. Avoid abbreviations (such as etc.) and slang (such as cool), and follow the standard rules of written English. Keep your tone formal.*

First, you must choose the topic of your research paper.

Your topic should be. . .

- ✔ something you find interesting
- ✔ something that has several sources written about it
- ✔ something your readers will find appealing
- ✔ the right size for the length of the assigned paper

Examples of Topics

Too Broad animals in Asia and Africa

Too Narrow the average height and weight of Asian and African elephants

Just Right the behaviors and lives of African and Asian elephants

> **Tip**
>
> *Make sure the sources you use are up-to-date; contain no grammatical, factual, or spelling errors; and seem trustworthy.*

After choosing your topic, begin gathering **details** from different sources. Try to gather a variety of details, including facts, quotations, and examples. To find the **sources** from which you will gather your details, you will need to **research.**

Begin your research by. . .

- ✔ going to the library and locating books related to your topic
- ✔ using several different search engines to locate websites with related information
- ✔ exploring any library databases available to you
- ✔ talking to teachers and librarians about your topic

Try to use as many different kinds of sources as possible. The more research you do and the more sources you locate, the better your paper will be. As you research, you will encounter both primary sources and secondary sources.

Definitions	Examples
Primary sources are original texts or documents that give firsthand knowledge.	diary, television interview, speech, autobiography, work of art, work of literature
A **secondary source** presents a writer's interpretation of information from a primary source.	reference work, biography, newspaper or magazine article, textbook

Tip

On your source cards, write

- *author's name*
- *title*
- *title of the magazine or newspaper if your source is an article*
- *page numbers if the source is a magazine; and page and section numbers if the source is a newspaper*
- *address and date you viewed it if it is an Internet article*
- *publisher's name*
- *date and place of publication*

Be sure to take notes as you research. Make a separate note card for each source.

On your note card, write. . .

✔ any details that you think might be useful for your paper

✔ the author's last name and the page number or numbers on which this information appears at the bottom of each note card

✔ a number in the upper right-hand corner for easy referencing

Record information about every source you read, even if you don't end up using information from that source. Record this information on **source cards.** You will use your source cards to create a **Works Cited** list at the end of your research paper. This is a list (in alphabetical order) of all the sources you cite in your paper.

Source Card for a Book

1

Redmond, Ian. Eyewitness: Elephant. New York:
DK Children, 2001.

Source Card for a Magazine

2

Siebert, Charles. "An Elephant Crackup?" New York Times Magazine. 8 Oct. 2006: 12–16.

Source Card for an Internet Reference Article

3

"Elephant." Encyclopædia Britannica. 2008. Encyclopædia Britannica Online. 21 Feb. 2008 <http://www.britannica.com/eb/article-9032357>.

After gathering details, plan your paper. Start by writing the **thesis statement.** Your thesis statement is more than just a restatement of the topic or of facts. It should state a specific point about the topic of your paper.

Strong Thesis Statement

Asian and African elephants are beautiful creatures that deserve our respect and protection.

Weak Thesis Statement

merely restates the topic

Asian and African elephants have very specific behaviors and ways of life.

Once you have written your thesis statement. . .

- ✔ think about the main points you will make in support of that idea
- ✔ return to your note cards and find details that support those main points
- ✔ organize your ideas into an outline

Your research paper is more than just a list of details. Ask yourself, "How do the details I have gathered from my sources relate to one another? How do they support the larger argument I am making?"

Sample Outline

Use Roman numerals to label main points and capital letters to label details.

If you have a point I, you must have a point II.

I. Asian and African elephants are extremely intelligent.
   A. Studies show that elephants have very good memories.
   B. Elephants communicate with each other.
   C. Elephants can use tools.

II. Elephants have complicated social lives.
   A. Elephants gather as a group to greet newborn members of the herd.
   B. Elephants grieve for their dead.
   C. Elephants can work together to accomplish goals.

The Three Parts of Your Paper

1. The **introduction,** which introduces your readers to your topic and major idea and grabs their attention
2. The **body,** which includes your main points and supporting details for each
3. The **conclusion,** which restates your major idea and leaves readers with a feeling of completeness

Activity A

Create a list of possible topics for a research paper. Then perform some preliminary research about one of those topics, using the methods recommended in this lesson. Record details from your research and information about your sources on index cards.

Activity B

Make an outline for the research paper you began in Activity A. Research more if you need to. Use the sample outline in this lesson as a model.

LESSON 4

Answer Essay Questions

On some tests, you may have to answer essay questions. The essay question (or writing prompt) will usually specify how long an essay you should write.

Tests are a fact of school life, so it is useful to learn as much as you can about them. In order to achieve the best possible result, there are certain steps you should follow no matter what kind of test you are taking.

Tip

Follow these steps not only on essay tests but also on multiple-choice tests, matching tests, fill-in-the-blank tests, or any other tests you might encounter.

Steps for Doing Your Best on Tests

1. Look over the whole test quickly to make sure you have seen all the parts and all the directions.
2. Estimate how much time you will need for each section.
3. For each part, take as much time as you need to read the directions slowly and more than once.
4. Study any examples, making sure you understand why the answer is marked as shown.
5. Start the first item when you are sure you know what to do.

An essay test is unlike a multiple-choice, short-answer, or matching test. An essay test requires a written answer as short as a few sentences or as long as several pages.

On an essay test. . .

✔ you must answer a specific question by writing a short essay
✔ you are not given possible answers to choose from
✔ the only resources you have are your own knowledge and writing skills

An essay question may ask you to. . .

✔ compare and contrast
✔ explain a process
✔ discuss causes and effects
✔ describe someone or something
✔ define a term
✔ express an opinion

Follow these steps when taking an essay test:

1. Read the essay prompt, or assignment, all the way through. Then reread, underlining the key words that tell you what you must do in your response.

> Name the two main characters in the story "The Wild West Show." Describe each one's physical appearance and personality.

2. Use the back of the test sheet or the margins to jot down notes about details you might want to include.
3. Decide which details to include, and make an informal outline to guide you as you write.
4. Draft your response.
5. Revise to make sure you have stuck to the topic and answered all the required parts of the question.
6. Edit and proofread for correct spelling, punctuation, grammar, and usage.

Because essay tests are usually timed, budget the amount of time you spend on each step. You should spend the longest amount of time drafting your response. Monitor yourself to make sure you stay on schedule. Also, remember the skills you have learned for writing essays.

Essay-writing Skills

- ✔ writing correct and interesting sentences
- ✔ developing a main idea or thesis statement, and writing a topic sentence
- ✔ making a plan to guide you as you write
- ✔ supporting your main idea
- ✔ choosing the best order in which to present your ideas
- ✔ writing a strong conclusion

The one-paragraph essay on the next page responds to the essay question "What is the moral of the traditional fairy tale 'Jack and the Beanstalk'?"

Sample Answer

The story "Jack and the Beanstalk" rewards greed and lying. Jack, its hero, is lazy, uncaring, and dishonest. He disobeys his mother by exchanging their cow for beans instead of selling it as she told him to. He does not thank the giant's wife, who saves him from the giant, but instead he chooses to steal from her husband. After returning, he and his mother are no longer poor and can live comfortably off the stolen golden goose eggs. But because he is greedy and ungrateful, Jack returns to the giant's home and steals more of their property. He does this not once but *twice*. At the end of the story, after lying, stealing, taking advantage of those who show him kindness, and murdering the rightful owner of the property he stole, he gets to marry a princess and live happily ever after. The moral of this fairy tale appears to be that those who commit crimes and show no concern for others deserve to be rewarded.

The writer uses specific examples from the story to prove his or her point.

Activity A

On a separate sheet of paper, prepare to answer the writing prompt below. Make sure you underline the key words in the question, gather your supporting details, and make a plan for writing.

Name and explain one change you wish could be made that would have a positive effect on your life or the lives of those around you. Discuss the effects this change would cause.

Activity B

Now, on a separate sheet, draft your answer to the essay question from Activity A.

WORKSHOP Writing Model

An excellent essay test answer...

- ✔ focuses exclusively on the question posed
- ✔ demonstrates your own knowledge and writing skills
- ✔ sticks to the topic and answers all parts of the question

Below is an essay test prompt and the complete response.

The prompt asks for the events in a cycle and for the student to draw a conclusion.

> **Prompt:** In one paragraph, describe the events of the water cycle and state why the water cycle is essential to life on Earth.
>
> The water cycle has two main events: evaporation and precipitation. In evaporation, water from oceans and rivers becomes warm enough to go into the atmosphere as water vapor. In precipitation, the water vapor in the atmosphere turns to liquid (rain) or solid (snow) and falls to Earth's surface. Between precipitation and evaporation, water flows over the ground or underground until it reaches a place where it can once again evaporate. The water cycle is essential to life because all living things need water to survive. Also, water helps plants grow. Plants are at the beginning of most food chains on Earth.

Assignment

Now write a response to one of the following essay test prompts. Make sure to answer each part of the question and stick to the subject.

Prompt: Choose an ancient civilization you have studied, such as ancient Greece or the ancient Maya. In one or two paragraphs, summarize how your own modern civilization is similar to and different from the ancient civilization you chose.

Prompt: In one or two paragraphs, describe the geography of your hometown. Be sure to include the major land and water features.

Writer's Handbook

CAPITALIZATION

- Capitalize the first word of a sentence and the pronoun *I*.

  That boy and I look alike.

- Capitalize the names of people, including their titles if the title appears before the name.

  Aunt Sarah

  Dr. Dina N. Gold

  Queen Elizabeth II

- Do not capitalize the name if it is used as a common noun.

  My uncle is a dentist.

- Capitalize the days of the week, months of the year, and holidays.

  Does Mother's Day fall on Sunday, May 8?

- Do not capitalize the names of the seasons.

  Finally, winter ended and spring began.

- Capitalize geographical names: cities, states, countries, continents, bodies of water, landmarks, and regions.

  We traveled to the Northeast and sailed on the Hudson River in New York State.

- Do not capitalize the name if it is used as a direction word.

  The state of Florida is south of Georgia.

- Capitalize the names of structures, streets, businesses, and organizations.

  The Department of Motor Vehicles is on Dell Avenue, past the Warner Bridge.

- Do not capitalize the name if it is used as a common noun:

  There is a busy highway behind our house.

- Capitalize the first, last, and important words of a title of a work, such as a book, story, song, movie, or painting. (Words that do not need to be capitalized include *a, an, and, or, of, to, for, by.)*

"The Most Embarrassing Moment of My Life"

A Proofread Sample

the hottest Day of last Summer was july 10. on that Day, my friends and I climbed mount monadnock. It is in the Southwestern part of new hampshire.

ABBREVIATIONS

An abbreviation is the short form of a word or phrase.

- Abbreviations of titles are acceptable in any type of writing.

Mr. (Mister)	**Dr. (Doctor)**

- Abbreviations for time are also acceptable in both formal and informal writing.

a.m. (*ante meridiem*)

p.m. (*post meridiem*)

- Do not use abbreviations of place names in formal writing.

U.S.A. or U.S. (United States of America)

CA (California)

St. (Street)

- Do not use abbreviations for measurements in formal writing.

km (kilometer)	**in. (inch)**
cm (centimeter)	**mi (mile)**

A Proofread Sample

Dr. New York
Doctor Perkins arrived in NY at
miles
9:30 am. He lives 2,000 mi away in
United Kingdom
the UK.

NUMBERS

- Numbers from zero to nine are usually written as words. Numbers 10 and over are usually written as numerals.

six	**60**

- Some large numbers are usually written with a combination of words and numerals.

8.3 million	**27 million**

- Always use words, not numerals, to begin a sentence.

  Thirteen students missed Monday's field trip.

- Use numerals to indicate amounts of money, decimals, percentages, chapters and pages, time, telephone numbers, dates, addresses, and statistics.

  $8.25 **July 4, 2009**

  12:43 p.m. **42 percent**

A Proofread Sample

> My sister is ~~6~~ six years old. She is ~~forty-four~~ 44 inches tall. ~~14~~ Fourteen friends came to her birthday party.

PUNCTUATION

End Marks

- Use a period to end most sentences (statements, mild commands or requests, and indirect questions).

  Help me, please.

  I do not know how to begin.

- Use a question mark to end a direct question.

  Why have you come?

  Where are you going?

- Use an exclamation point only after a strong command, a sentence that expresses excitement, or an exclamation.

  Close the door!

  I couldn't believe my eyes!

  How wonderful! Yikes!

A Proofread Sample

> Did somebody ring the doorbell! ? I wondered who it could be? . I opened the door! , ~~I~~t was my Uncle Theo? . What a shock? !

Apostrophes

- Add an apostrophe and *-s* to show possession by a singular noun (one owner).

  Madison's hair is red, like her father's.

- Add just an apostrophe to show possession by a plural noun (more than one owner).

  The neighbors' dogs are in the Donovans' yard.

- Add an apostrophe and *-s* to show possession by a plural noun that does not end with *s*.

  Geese's honks came from the children's room.

- Use an apostrophe to stand for missing letters in contractions.

  I'm sure I wouldn't do that if I were you. (I am; would not)

- Do not use an apostrophe to show possession with most pronouns.

  That labrador is hers.

  Which jars filled with pennies are theirs?

A Proofread Sample

Mitch Saltzman has been invited to three ~~party's~~ parties. He can attend only one friend's party. He will probably go to Jason's party because it's closest to the Saltzmans' home.

Commas

- Use commas to separate three or more items in a series.

  Lunch was an egg, a salad, and an apple juice.

- Use a comma to separate two or more adjectives before a noun if the adjectives modify, or describe, the same noun.

  Taste one of these crisp, sweet apples.

- Use a comma before a conjunction in a compound sentence (complete sentences joined by *and*, *but*, or *or*).

  The day turned hot, and we hoped to go swimming.

- Use a comma after an introductory phrase.

  Living on the mountain, goats must be sure-footed.

- Use commas to separate an appositive from the rest of the sentence. (An appositive is a noun or noun phrase that identifies a pronoun or another noun in the sentence.)

  Mr. Ramirez, the algebra teacher, found his missing coat.

- Use commas to set off any group of words that offers additional information.

  Thomas Jefferson, who was an inventor as well as a statesman, designed his own home.

- Use commas to set off the name of someone being addressed.

  I am glad to hear you're feeling better, Uncle Warren.

- Use commas to set off *yes*, *no*, and other interrupters and transition words.

  No, the secret was not kept.

  The thief, of course, had disappeared.

- Use commas to separate elements of addresses and dates.

The framers of the United States Constitution met in Philadelphia, Pennsylvania, from May 17, 1787, until the end of that summer.

A Proofread Sample

> The beautiful, welcoming city of San Francisco, California, is always in danger from earthquakes. The worst one so far, which had a magnitude of 8.3 on the Richter scale, lasted two days in April, 1906. Hundreds of people died.

- See the chart below for rules about when not to use a comma.

Semicolons

- Use a semicolon to separate two complete sentences that are closely connected in meaning (and not joined by *and*, *but*, or *or*).

He practiced the piano three hours each afternoon; he did not give up sports, however.

A Proofread Sample

> The main ingredients are flour, sugar, butter, and spices; nuts and bananas may also be added.

Colons

- Use a colon to introduce a list.

Listen to the noisy seashore: crashing waves, screeching gulls, and whistling wind.

Do not use commas. . .	Example
between adjectives that should stay together. If the adjectives make sense separated by *and*, insert the comma. If they sound odd, leave out the comma.	**This gleaming red car has plush leather seats.**
if an appositive is necessary to the meaning of the sentence.	**The statesman Thomas Jefferson also designed buildings.**
if a phrase or clause contains necessary information.	**The home that Jefferson designed is called Monticello.**
if only the month and year of a date are named.	**The Constitutional Convention lasted until September 1787.**

- Do not use a colon after an introduction unless that introduction is a complete sentence.

  Listen to the seashore noises of crashing waves, screeching gulls, and whistling wind.

  A Proofread Sample

  The speakers are: Jaden, Vanessa, and Haley. These are the topics they will talk about: bicycle safety, first aid, and sports safety.

Punctuating Dialogue

Use quotation marks, other punctuation marks, and capital letters to show dialogue (the exact words of characters or people). Indent a paragraph each time the speaker changes.

- If the speaker is named first, put a comma before the opening quotation marks, and capitalize the first word of the speech. Put a period or other end mark inside the closing quotation marks.

  Sophie said, "There's something strange about this room."

- If the speech is given first, put the end mark inside the closing quotation marks.

  "Are you scared?" asked Roger.

- If the speech is interrupted, enclose each part within quotation marks. The second part of the speech is not capitalized.

  "I get the funny feeling that we're not alone," Emma agreed, "and it makes me uncomfortable."

  A Proofread Sample

  "What are you doing this summer?" asked Mo. Ann replied, "I am visiting Utah." "I'm playing soccer," Mo said, "with my friends."

Punctuating Titles

- Use quotation marks to enclose titles of short works, such as short stories, articles, chapters, poems, and songs.

  Our class read the story "Papa's Parrot" by Cynthia Rylant.

- Use underlining or italic type for titles of longer works, such as books, magazines, newspapers, movies, and plays.

  I enjoyed the book *Charlotte's Web*.

  A Proofread Sample

  The musical "My Fair Lady" features the song I Could Have Danced All Night.

SPELLING

Adding Endings

- For most words, just add the ending without making spelling changes.

  jump + -ed = jumped

  rain + -ing = raining

- If a one-syllable word ends with a consonant preceded by a single vowel, and the ending begins with a vowel, double the final consonant. If the word has more than one syllable, double the final consonant only if the last syllable is stressed.

  big + -est = biggest

  begin + -er = beginner

  limit + -ed = limited

- If the word ends with a final silent *e*, and the ending begins with a vowel, drop the final *e*. Keep the final *e* if the ending begins with a consonant.

  hope + -ing = hoping

  hope + -ful = hopeful

- If the word ends with a consonant and *y*, and the ending begins with any letter except *i*, change the *y* to *i*. If the word ends with a vowel and *y*, just add the ending.

  try + -ed = tried

  play + -ful = playful

A Proofread Sample

Larissa was chooseing a stuffd pet. She was haveing trouble decideing between the fury bear and the cuddley kitten. She cryed out with happyness when she saw the pig.

Making Plurals

- To make most nouns plural, add *-s*.

days	**zoos**

- If the noun ends with *s*, *ss*, *sh*, *ch*, *zz*, or *x*, add *-es*.

kisses	**boxes**
lunches	**matches**

- If the noun ends with a consonant and *y*, change the *y* to *i*, and add *-es*.

city/cities	**fly/flies**

- For some nouns, change a final *f* or *fe* to *ves*.

shelf/shelves	**life/lives**
knife/knives	**leaf/leaves**

- Some nouns change spellings in singular and plural forms.

tooth/teeth	**man/men**
foot/feet	**woman/women**
mouse/mice	**child/children**

- Some nouns keep the same spelling in singular and plural forms.

deer **pants** **sheep** **scissors**

A Proofread Sample

mice
The ~~mouses~~ hid behind the bookes on the shelfs. Only their tailes showed.

Tricky Letter Combinations

- Remember to put *i* before *e* except after *c*, or when it sounds like a long *a* as in *neighbor* or *weigh*. This rhyme may also help you remember whether to spell *ie* or *ei*: "*i* before *e* except after *c* when sounded as *ee*."

believe	niece	weigh	field
receive	piece	thief	brief
neighbor	ceiling		

Exceptions

friend	weird	either	neither
species	protein	seize	

- Consult a dictionary or the lists below when deciding among *-er*, *-or*, and *-ar*.

-er (most common)	-or	-ar (least common)
answer	actor	calendar
brother	color	collar
enter	doctor	dollar
weather	motor	sugar

A Proofread Sample

The docter recieved a calendor that cost fifty dollers and put it in her breifcase. Its auther is her brothar.

Commonly Misspelled Words

- These words cause confusion mostly because writers may not remember whether to use one or two consonants in them.

accidentally	during	occurrence
accommodate	embarrass	opportunity
address	exaggerate	possession
already	generally	professional
balloon	hoping	recommend
basically	immediately	succeed
beginning	necessary	success
committee	occasionally	tomorrow
disappointed	occur	vacuum
discuss	occurred	welcome

A Proofread Sample

If you wish to suceed, I reccommend that you find a new oportunnity imediately.

COMMON USAGE ERRORS

Look for these errors in your writing (and listen for them in your speech). Try to correct them.

Should have, would have, could have

- "They should of been here hours ago." Do not use *of* after *should*, *could*, and *would*. The correct verb forms are *should have*, *could have*, *would have*.

Avoid Double Negatives

- "He didn't do nothing wrong." Do not use two negative words together to emphasize the negative. These are correct usages: "He didn't do anything wrong"; "He did nothing wrong."

Lay, Lie

- "I want to lay down for a nap." Do not use *lay* when you mean *lie*.

  Compare the verbs and their forms in the chart below.

A Proofread Sample

> Danielle shouldn't ~~of~~ have been laying in the sun without ~~no~~ sunscreen.

Subject-Verb Agreement

The subject and the verb in a sentence must agree in number. A singular subject needs a singular verb, and a plural subject needs a plural verb. Most singular verbs in the present tense end in –s or –es.

The teacher stands by the board.

The students sit at their desks.

- The subject of a sentence may be either a noun or a pronoun.
  - Singular pronouns: *I*, *you*, *he*, *she*, and *it*
  - Plural pronouns: *you*, *we*, *they*

  She plays soccer in the spring.

  They play football in the fall.

Lay and Lie

Verb	Present Participle	Past Tense	Past Participle	Examples
lie ("to rest or recline"; does not take an object)	lying	lay	(has) lain	The dog wants to lie down. It lay sleeping on its blanket. It has lain there all morning.
lay ("to place or set"; *laying* takes an object)	laying	laid	(has) laid	Workers are coming to lay the carpet. They laid carpet in one room yesterday.

A Proofread Sample

I eats a sandwich for lunch. Then Sam and I walks to class.

Common Pronoun Usage

- Personal pronouns take different forms if they are the subject or object within a sentence.

Subject	Object
I	me
he	him
she	her
we	us
they	them

He ran two miles.

Jenny mailed him a birthday card.

- **Note:** *You* and *it* are the same as both subject and object.

A Proofread Sample

She her
~~Her~~ went to the mall with ~~she~~
They
mother. ~~Them~~ shopped for school clothes.

Modifiers

Adjectives and adverbs are words used to describe, or modify, other words.

Adjectives

- Proper adjectives are formed from proper nouns. They are always capitalized.

  The Japanese outfielder became very popular with fans.

- Adjectives formed from common nouns are not capitalized.

  She walked down the dusty street.
  It was a beautiful day.

Adverbs

- An adverb is a word that modifies a verb, an adjective, or another adverb. Many adverbs, but not all, end in *–ly*.

  Navin works very quickly.

A Proofread Sample

cold
Friday was an ~~coldly~~ day. Ana ran
ly
quick all the way home.

Index